We Can Speak for Ourselves

BREAKTHROUGHS IN THE SOCIOLOGY OF EDUCATION

Volume 5

Series Editor:

George W. Noblit, *Joseph R. Neikirk Distinguished Professor of Sociology of Education, University of North Carolina at Chapel Hill, USA*

In this series, we are establishing a new tradition in the sociology of education. Like many fields, the sociology of education has largely assumed that the field develops through the steady accumulation of studies. Thomas Kuhn referred to this as 'normal science.' Yet normal science builds on a paradigm shift, elaborating and expanding the paradigm. What has received less attention are the works that contribute to paradigm shifts themselves. To remedy this, we will focus on books that move the field in dramatic and recognizable ways—what can be called breakthroughs.

Kuhn was analyzing natural science and was less sure his ideas fit the social sciences. Yet it is likely that the social sciences are more subject to paradigm shifts than the natural sciences because the social sciences are fed back into the social world. Thus sociology and social life react to each other, and are less able separate the knower from the known. With reactivity of culture and knowledge, the social sciences follow a more complex process than that of natural science. This is clearly the case with the sociology of education. The multiplicity of theories and methods mix with issues of normativity—in terms of what constitutes good research, policy and/or practice. Moreover, the sociology of education is increasingly global in its reach—meaning that the national interests are now less defining of the field and more interrogative of what is important to know. This makes the sociology of education even more complex and multiple in its paradigm configurations. The result is both that there is less shared agreement on the social facts of education but more vibrancy as a field. What we know and understand is shifting on multiple fronts constantly. Breakthroughs is to the series for works that push the boundaries—a place where all the books do more than contribute to the field, they remake the field in fundamental ways. Books are selected precisely because they change how we understand both education and the sociology of education.

We Can Speak for Ourselves

Parent Involvement and Ideologies of Black Mothers in Chicago

Billye Sankofa Waters
Northeastern University, Boston, USA

SENSE PUBLISHERS
ROTTERDAM/BOSTON/TAIPEI

A C.I.P. record for this book is available from the Library of Congress.

ISBN: 978-94-6300-269-1 (paperback)
ISBN: 978-94-6300-270-7 (hardback)
ISBN: 978-94-6300-271-4 (e-book)

Published by: Sense Publishers,
P.O. Box 21858,
3001 AW Rotterdam,
The Netherlands
https://www.sensepublishers.com/

All chapters in this book have undergone peer review.

Cover image: Because I Am Free, by Joyce Owens (2012)

Printed on acid-free paper

ADVANCE PRAISE FOR
WE CAN SPEAK FOR OURSELVES

We Can Speak for Ourselves contributes new insight and pushes established ideas into broader contexts. Sankofa Waters uses a compilation of theories and data sources to provide a unique exploration of the Black mothering experience and the relevance of such in current U.S. society. The research is a solid contribution to this body of knowledge and beautifully unifies a wide range of contextual issues that are salient to the Black community and beyond.
Rhonda Jeffries – University of South Carolina; author of *Performance Traditions Among African-American Teachers* and co-editor of *Black Women in the Field: Experiences Understanding Ourselves and Others through Qualitative Research*

We Can Speak for Ourselves is a necessary read for everyone, especially Black mothers, who are on the front lines of the Black Lives Matter Movement. After all, the movement at its core is about resisting the anti-Black society in which Black mothers are forced to raise their children. Sankofa Waters beautifully blends personal writings, counternarratives, and the voices of five Black mothers to create a book that gives us new language to address the issues impacting Black families and Black survival. Through this work, Sankofa Waters expertly depicts the struggles of Black mothers as organic intellectuals deconstructing, critiquing, and navigating the power structures that oppress their sons, daughters, and Black communities at large.
Bettina L. Love – University of Georgia; Board Chair of The Kindezi School in Atlanta, Georgia; 2016 Nasir Jones Fellow at the W. E. B. Du Bois Research Institute at Harvard University; and author of *Hip Hop's Li'l Sistas Speak: Negotiating Hip Hop Identities and Politics in the New South*

Through the captivating counternarratives of Black mothers in Chicago, Sankofa Waters brilliantly challenges preconceived notions of what it means to be both a mother and an involved parent in urban schools. *We Can Speak for Ourselves* offers voices of resilience, faith, and hope as Black mothers navigate the dynamics of race, class, and gender in their quest to provide a quality education for their children. This is a must read for educators, scholars, and activists who believe that the lives of Black children do, in fact, matter.
Paula Groves Price – Washington State University; Associate Dean of Diversity and International Programs and Editor in Chief of the *Western Journal of Black Studies*

The brilliantly insightful Dr. Sankofa Waters draws upon extensive qualitative and participatory research to explore the ways that Black mothers come to know and participate in their children's education. *We Can Speak for Ourselves* plumbs Black feminist epistemology and critical theory to create a new model that reimagines the critical terrain of both public and private African American female 'motherwork.' It is intersectionally deft in how it attends to both structural issues of inequality and intragroup negotiation of identity. This book is bold, well-researched and an important contribution to the fields of Education, Sociology, Women's and Gender Studies and Public Policy.

Michele Berger – University of North Carolina, Chapel Hill; author of *Workable Sisterhood: The Political Journey of Stigmatized Women with HIV/AIDS* and co-author of *Transforming Scholarship: Why Women's and Gender Studies Students are Changing Themselves and the World*

Billye Sankofa Waters reiterates the plaintive lament of the mothers of 1970s Boston when they said, 'When we fight about education we're fighting for our lives.' This story of parents in Chicago is powerful, poignant, and oh so familiar. This is a must read!

Gloria Ladson-Billings – University of Wisconsin, Madison; Kellner Family Professor of Urban Education; author of *The Dreamkeepers: Successful Teachers of African American Children* and *Crossing Over to Canaan: The Journey of New Teachers in Diverse Classrooms*

This book is the product of an 8-year process that began when I left Chicago to pursue "higher" education. My mother and I started on the road to Chapel Hill but after about two hours in to the drive, Cousin Eric called to inform us her mother/my grandmother passed away. We double backed to Chicago to repack bags, after which my mother insisted upon completing the initial drive with me. She drove the entire 12 hours before I boarded her on a plane to Galveston, Texas to pay her last respects to our family matriarch – and to assume her role as such. Along those highways I accepted that my grandmother took the road ahead to guide my journey. However, it was never clearer until I completed and submitted this first full manuscript – on the day of her birth, 2015. I realize she has been writing this with me the entire time.

Zola Luetta Jones Temple
(February 1, c.1913 – August 5, 2007)

TABLE OF CONTENTS

FOREWORD

Through a blend of personal writing and academic research, *We Can Speak for Ourselves* is a multifaceted analysis of the ways in which society conceptualizes Black mothers. Negative portrayals continue to permeate film, music, and other forms of media; Black women are often over-sexualized and under intellectualized in academic scholarship. Billye stands with a community of mothers to *push back* while highlighting various levels of agency Black mothers engage to move forward. This work bridges seminal Black feminist writings and is in conversation with the contemporary work of motherhood and women's studies (see Camille Wilson, Robin Boylorn, Kaila Adia Story), which explores "motherhood as praxis, institution, and lived experience" (Story, 2014, p. 1). This book highlights the grave conditions facing Black mothers and articulates a new viewpoint of Black women's lives and capabilities. This book asserts their narratives as empirical data and is critical in nature because it is a call to action.

This book provides a passenger-side view of a project that moved beyond a 10-week work assignment to evolve as a multi-generation chronicle of resistance work, which challenges the dominant understandings of Black mothers in American society. *We Can Speak for Ourselves* is rooted in the everyday lives of Black mothers and contributions to their communities that include children, partners, cousins, stepparents, godparents, Big Mama, neighbors, and teachers. These stories reinforce the scholarship of Black motherwork, which is often not regarded as activism and require us as a collective people to engage dialogue that recognizes Black women's contributions across time and space. Billye offers a poignant historical analysis of controlling images alongside an intricate analysis of contemporary issues in popular culture. More importantly she – along with the mothers of this project who are acknowledged as co-participants – challenge the pervasive assumptions about Black women and their approaches to mothering and care.

It is an honor and privilege – as a Black mother, a Chicago native, a village daughter, and a sister-scholar – to pen the foreword for such a timely collection of work. I have walked alongside Billye as a poet, mentor, and work with her as both a university colleague and community activist on behalf of Black women, girls, and social justice. We are partners in the struggle to re-present Black women's lived experiences, specifically within Education and Women's Studies. Our research and practice are always intimate and intersectional. When the former is called into question as me-search, we understand the urgency to create *more* space for the voices we have heard our entire lives – praying, laughing, crying, affirming. *We speak* because so many have lost their voices screaming or were buried in fear and tragedy, and this silence has rendered invisibility. This work is a celebration of voices – all voices. This work is an important piece of an immutable patchwork that collectively advances equitable rights and resources for Black mothers and children.

Kristal Moore Clemons, Ph.D.

PREFACE

This book was birthed from my dissertation studies and before that, the desire to honor the mothers I have known and seen my entire life. I understand this with clear hindsight. What you are reading has gone through dozens upon dozens of word-for-word, line-by-line revisions as if every single letter were a tool all by itself, and a grand committee of peer and senior reviewers. However, this was not my first choice for a project.

When I began graduate school, I showed up in my advisor's office every week with a new idea – each one more elaborately passionate than the one before. I'd taken a 60% pay cut to leave a position I loved and moved 765 miles south – past the Mason-Dixon line – so this work had to mean something. The problem is, I wanted it to mean *everything* and my wheels spun around a world of lifelong projects that I thought I could complete in five academic years. That first year of the program the only question that seemed to matter was "what are your research claims?" I would rattle off anything between "philosophy and literature of the Harlem Renaissance" to "teacher prep in urban classrooms."

The final semester of my Master's program, I enrolled in *Schooling versus Education of African American Students in K-12 Public Education* with Dr. Eileen Parsons. This course gave me the language of *culturally relevant pedagogy* and *critical race theory* and my world exploded. Finally, I could understand the connections between theory and practice as activist dimensions and I diligently committed the work of Gloria Ladson-Billings, Derrick Bell, Mwalimu Shujaa, and John Stanfield to memory. In fact, I was so enthusiastically ambitious that I claimed *critical race theory* as one of my research areas and for this reason Dr. Parsons mercilessly pushed me beyond my learning edge.

The previous semester I'd enrolled in *Theorizing Black Feminisms* with Dr. Michele Berger. I died a little on the inside every time I earned a "B" on an assignment. I'd pour out tens of thousands of words over the course of those 16 weeks. I added dozens of new names across centuries of history, and countless hours – even in my sleep and nightmares of violence against Black women. And all I could get was a B, as in "do better"? I was a bit angry.

So I humbled myself and dug deeper. I attended office hours and read more. I had discussions with other colleagues to refine and bolster my ideas. I submitted articles and conference papers on critical race theory, qualitative research, and Black feminism across disciplines to receive even more critical feedback. I began to appreciate Parsons and Berger immensely while learning that the goal was/is never "Mastery" but "growth." One of the most indescribable moments was attending the

National Women's Studies Association 2009 annual conference. My sister-mentor Kristal Clemons told me to jump in the car, and we headed to Atlanta. I was floored that all my teachers – Paula Giddings, Angela Davis, Johnnetta B. Cole, Kimberlé Crenshaw… were walking around as my living and breathing textbooks that I could approach and learn from in real life.

There is so much beauty in that I have been learning critical race theory and Black feminism as I both live and write it – when I thought it had to be the other way around. This work allows me to touch my history every day, and I honor this responsibility.

And when I began to move toward my dissertation, and someone referred to me as the "Black mother expert" I cringed. Hard. It was wrong. I was not a Black mother (by biological definition), and I was not an expert. That was a box that felt limiting and completely misassigned. I was most uncomfortable with the assertion that of all my research interests, "Black mothers" would be the only one I would be asked about. I was uncomfortable until I fully began to understand Black motherhood as an incredibly expansive identity; it allows me to understand the toughest and most vulnerable parts of myself. It allows me to critique interlocking systems of oppression and develop spaces for reciprocity and healing (Dillard, 2000, 2008). It allows me to excavate dynamic stories and build collages that claim futures for my children and grandchildren. It allows me to create homes wherever I go and to speak freely in a dialect that is both familiar and empirical. Therefore, when I began writing this, one of the greatest joys was that I was able to return to Chicago and do this with my family. I composed drafts of my analysis while sitting with my mother and the biggest compliment I've ever received is: "I can read this."

I write for Jeffery Manor and everyone on the block who asks, "when's the next book coming? You gotta write about us." I write for State Street: because I went to Beasley on 52nd, my father taught at DuSable on 49th and my mother taught at Beethoven on 47th – all under the shadows of the demolished Robert Taylor Housing Projects – and new prospect for the Obama Presidential Library. I write for my Sorors from 1913 to present. I write for my classmates at Olive Harvey who felt like they hit a dead end. I write for the 19-year old girl who left Howard University with a .08 GPA. I write for my sisters and brothers in the academy who are still the first, few, and only. I write for my mama and 'nem, Grandma Eva and 'nem, my family in Cameroon, the Queen Mother and Kings 'nem. I write for the times I sat in the middle of my bed feeling paralyzed with the fear of high expectations and screaming to God to let the words just fall out of my head onto the paper or screen because I swore through desperate tears that I had nothing left (and it happened) – and for every person who tells me they experience the same. I write this for every sister circle, fish fry, game night, sleepover, kitchen table study group, touch-and-agreeing affirmation I was blessed with to get through graduate school. I write for my doc students who want to change the world chapter by chapter. I write for my public and charter school students who want to change the world block by block. I write for my partner who read one of my first Black feminist assignments "Coming Apart" by

Alice Walker with me because I didn't want to feel stupid when I discussed it in class with people I thought knew more than me. I write for the homeland umbilical cord that was severed so that I may contribute to the healing of our conscious identity. I write for the Rhodes' the Temple's the Jones' the Barnett's the Njoya's the unborn and unclaimed sankofawaters'. I write for my student who sat in a teacher prep course and had to listen to an instructor explain how to prepare herself to teach in urban environments with Black mothers as a curricular battle plan. I write because Chicago is changing, and I don't want it to, but we all have to grow up. I write because the world is changing, and I need it to because I want my kids to grow up. I write for my healing. I write for the warriors with crippled with arthritis, dementia, deferred dreams, broken hearts, and wounded egos. I write for the warriors who trust me with the baton. I write for people who don't read "academic" books, but may pick this up – and may even keep reading because they see/hear/feel my heart.

This is not a book of solutions. This is a book of stories. This is a book of love. We go on record.

RATIONALE FOR THIS BOOK

According to Comer and Haynes (1991), American education fails to address needs of Black children largely because the structure of public education and the philosophies that guide its development neglect salient features of Black culture and life. In other words, most schools are not culturally responsive to Black families and do not engage their knowledge and lived experiences. This book does not propose a mandate or sanction a specific program that may facilitate the goals of educators, researchers, and policymakers to align with Black families. Instead, it departs from the work of seminal/conventional sociology such as Bronislaw Malinowski (1926, 1927) and Sander Gilman (1985) that has been performed on Black bodies, to open a space within these varied discourses – specifically for Black mothers to speak for themselves rather than be spoken for.

This ethnographic project is an intervention of self-representation that explores experiences of five Black mothers of the same Chicago elementary school with respect to their relationship with the author – a qualitative researcher – over a period of two years. Black feminist epistemology (Hill-Collins, 1989/1995) is the framework that directed this project, fieldwork, and interpretation of the findings to better examine the perceptions brought through the everyday consumption of controlling images that help to "justify U.S. Black women's oppression" (Hill-Collins, 2004a, p. 47). This work employs tools of poetry (Lorde, 1977/2007) and counternarratives, a widely understood component of Critical Race Theory (CRT) which "aims to cast doubt on the validity of accepted premises or myths, especially ones held by the majority" (Delgado & Stefancic, 2001, p. 144). Additionally, the work of D. Soyini Madison (2005) is explored with respect to reflexivity to consider broader meanings for operations of the human condition; and how this work makes the greatest contribution to equity, freedom, and justice.

We Can Speak for Ourselves examines Scientific, Government, Feminist/ Mothering, Education, and Popular Media discourses to underscore the historical trajectory in which Black mothers are currently scrutinized and speak back to. Four themes guide the analysis; three name a specific action with a specific stakeholder: Defining Mother, Preparing Children, Navigating Institution, while the fourth, named Other – discusses the complexities of mothers who are further marginalized by class and intragroup expectations. The voices of this project are urgent, particularly in a time where there are competing societal goals for global access and basic survival in the so-called murder capitals (Johnson, 2013) of America. These narratives require all those concerned with the care and high expectations of our children to look within, across, and beyond systems to actively engage discourse that is multilingual and inclusive. From this space, we co-create action agendas and leverage networks of power, which situate Black mothers and children as key stakeholders rather than subjects of inquiry.

An Epilogue is provided to discuss the emergence of violence that has occurred since this project formally concluded in early 2012. Current issues are explored with respect to a historical lens; social media as a literature source; maps for further research; and challenges to multiple audiences.

AUDIENCES FOR THIS BOOK

Sociologists.   Previous works describe the role of both Black women and mothers as an imperative catalyst to a destabilized society based on primitive [*sic*] and dysfunctional norms (see *Crime and Custom in Savage Society*, 1926; *Sex and Repression in Savage Society*, 1927; *Losing Ground: American Social Policy 1950–1980*, 1984; *Difference and Pathology: Stereotypes of Sexuality, Race, and Madness*, 1985). This book critiques and departs from conventional sociology to provide nuanced perspectives of Black women – in their voices – inserting/asserting their expertise on identity and family. This project specifically speaks to the motherwork of Black women, which influences positive self-image and restorative justice projects, which are an urgent concern given the current climate of violence and disenfranchisement in our major cities.

Sociologists of education.   Many Sociologists of Education are concerned with issues of race, class, and gender. This work not only addresses broader issues of racism as the interplay of race with class and gender, but it discusses issues related to schooling specifically. The narratives of these women contribute to the discourses of culturally relevant pedagogy (Ladson-Billings, 1995) and leadership.

Qualitative researchers.   As a "postcritical ethnographer" (Noblit, Flores, & Murillo. Jr., 2004), this work adopts a new paradigm approach for analysis, interpretation, and writing. This approach, within qualitative inquiry, is framed by the work of D. Soyini Madison (2011) who defines critical ethnography as social justice and risk coupled with truth and translation. Much like the reciprocal relationship between parents and teachers, she asks that the same take place between the researchers and participants with an essential focus on the reflexivity of the researcher.

Feminist educators and researchers. Employing a feminist methodology was/is critical because of its commitment to social justice. A feminist method in sociology research works to dismantle power structures and recognizes that women experience oppression and exploitation based on race, class, and sexual orientation much differently than others (Reinharz, 1992). Taking steps further, "involving much more than simply the counseling of existing social sciences, the placing of ideas and experiences of women of color in the center of analysis requires invoking a different epistemology" (Hill-Collins, 2004a, p. 49).

Black women/mothers/othermothers. It is important to note that while the voices of these women are shared to speak to an academic audience, they are also speaking back to themselves; the data chapter centralizes the women's voices and thus are broadly accessible. It is important the participants of this project see themselves as major contributors to a body of work that speaks to, for, about, and with them.

Social justice educators. This work speaks to all educators interested in issues of equity in education, particularly that within urban areas.

ACKNOWLEDGEMENTS

I am grateful that God enables me to use my gifts of writing, my passion for education, and my community of Black mothers/fathers, men/women, to not only facilitate the writing of this book, but to inform every step – from birth until present. Years ago I wrote a line in a poem: "I am jealous of the woman I am yet to become." However, I am so grateful to be in the presence of mind to excitedly accept the woman I am right now. Not because this journey is complete but because this journey has taught me to fight. This journey has taught me to be still. This journey has taught me to exhaust all possibilities. This journey has taught me to ask for help. Through this journey, I have grown roots strong and deep. Thank you, Father God for making it clear that you will in *all ways* prepare me and I can rest/rejoice in knowing that each and *every* journey *is* the blessing.

I am grateful for my first teacher – my mother – Mary Rhodes. Thank you for listening attentively to every draft, every question, every brainstorm. I count it a triple blessing that not only did this project teach me more about myself as a Black woman and gave you tools to see your phenomenal work as an othermother, it created a beautiful comradery between us. You called to share books, news reports, and stories of our family I had never heard before. You have proudly relished in how I have grown as a woman; however, you are the foundation for all that I am. I am proud to relish in your revelations as a feminist and friend.

I am grateful for my best friend, Malari. You have walked every step with me since we met in Harlem – allowing me to grow as a scholar, a woman, an artist, and a life partner. You have been my wake-up call, my assistant researcher, my personal trainer, my comedian, and my resting place – teaching me the greatest lessons in effective communication and how to support a freedom fighter.

I am grateful for Kristal. You were a sister the first day I met you. Thank you for introducing me to myself – as a Black feminist. Thank you for believing, challenging, supporting, and laughing. Thank you for investing in me with your intellect and your spirit. Thank you for driving to Chicago at midnight. You have shown me the rewards of self-determination, faith, and excellence. Thank you for sharing the work our souls must have.

I am grateful for Renée. You are an awesome big sister. You make it look so easy, and I am more grateful and humbled that you have taken the time to show me life behind the veil. Because of your example, I have grown confident to walk as professor, artist, wife, and mother. Thank you for reintroducing me to "playtime." Additionally, thank you, Howard for introducing me to her and you both for sharing Brother Bakari with me.

I am grateful for George. I excelled because of your foresight, your candor, your advocacy, and the community of scholars you have raised to create a cross-cultural, cross-country network of intellectual activism. You keep me reminded that I am an artist – first – which is one of my greatest tools for social justice. Your explosive laughter, hugs, and thoughtful probing have created a safe space, ripe for love and agency.

I am grateful for Shanyce. You are the balance; the one who is on when I am off; the one who can present the rational argument when the whole world is irrational; the one with whom I can end a 3-hour conversation and pick the phone right back up because there was still one more point to make; the one who can get a prayer through a million brick walls and I never have to ask.

I am grateful for my Chapel Hill/Critical Conference Sisters: Dr. Jessie, Dr. Dani, Dr. Karla, Dr. Corliss, Dr. Cassandra, Dr. Shannon. We did it! Each of you has provided amazing support beyond the academy – across dinner tables, marriage celebrations, church services, Bimbe festivals through Charlotte, Pittsburgh, Brooklyn, Toronto, Puerto Rico. I have been able to call on you at the last minute and sometimes every day. I am challenged by your individual/our collective projects and thrilled we travel the world doing what we love. Your friendship has extended my family.

I am grateful for Howard University. You introduced me to my Bamoun cousin and life pledge brother Glenn NSangou; Elle, who I have been blessed to watch evolve into the most beautiful of butterflies; Kea Iman, who shared her faith and allowed me to flourish; and The Samuels – Dre and Trinishia – the ultimate Big Brother and Big Sister.

I am grateful for Cassie, my Dolphin Soror Bee and MaToya, my "Mom." You have introduced me to a sisterhood beyond the oaths and doctrines. You allowed me to discover and be my FULL self. And stayed. And talked mess. And let me talk mess back. And Janine, and Safiya, and Dot, and Nicole always chime in. And we've never missed a beat.

I am grateful for Nieal Marie Smith. Beasley. William and Tyler. Mary and Mary Anna. Paducah. Twenty-nine years. Period.

I am grateful for Don and Antwan. You have been my protectors and champions since Day 1.

I am grateful for Uncle Daniel T. Parker; you adopted me with open arms. Thank you for introducing me to Sister Joyce Owens, who graciously contributed her work to this book. Additionally, thank you Brother Khalid el-Hakim for digging through your crates as well.

I am grateful for my older brothers Preston and Aaron, and younger sister DaChé – of whom I am immensely proud of and inspired by.

I am grateful for my Sorors of Delta Sigma Theta with an abundance of violets to the most magnificent Lambda Chapter; Natalie, Andrea, Dymeme, Micki, Jenny from the block, Chim, Terica Terica Terica, Krystal Blue like the lake, B9 – my front, Shontay – my back, Jamie "Caston" from Loyola, Sherry Stephens, and Ngozi; and the Chicago Alumnae Chapter.

I am grateful for my Othermothers and Sisters who were instrumental to this work and my life throughout this process: The women of the Temple/Rhodes families; Mary A. Leonard, Claudine Andrews, Shawn Arango Ricks, Shemariah Arki, Kimya Barden, Denise Taliaferro Baszile, Vicki Behrens, Theodora Regina Berry, Silvia Bettez, Sheree Boyd, Robin Boylorn, Lisa Brock, Malika Butler, Michelle Clayborn, Deirdre Cobb-Roberts, Daniella Cook, Sarah Jane Quessa Coupet, Sheryl Cozart, Deb Eaker Rich, Venus Evans-Winters, Tracy Fletcher, Daris Frencha, Gretchen Givens Generett, Jocelyn Glazier, Dana Griffin, Beth Hatt, Deborah Harris, Terry Houston, Blair L. M. Kelley, April Knox, Rhonda Lewis, Roxanne London, Ollie McLemore, D. Soyini Madison, Hattie Mukombe, Dara Nix-Stevenson, Stella Norman, Eileen Parsons, Marya Sherron, Stephanie Shonekan, Tracy Smith-Jackson, Mary Stone Hanley, Gigi Taylor, Linda Tillman, Regina Townsend, Wanda Tyndall-White, Karolyn Tyson, Sofia Villenas, Angie and Imani Walker, Lydia Williams.

I am especially grateful to Rhonda Jeffries, Bettina Love, Paula Groves Price, Michele Berger and Gloria Ladson-Billings. I am humbled a thousand times over by your investment, affirmation, suggestions, and corrections to this book manuscript – and especially for your willingness to serve as a big sister.

I am grateful for my Otherfathers and Brothers who were instrumental to this work and my life throughout this process: The men of the Temple/Rhodes families, my father in particular – William N. Rhodes; Darrell Cleveland, Willie Dixon, Thomas Green, Sam Greenlee, Denis Gully, Jake Jacobs, Mike Jennings, David J. Leonard, Richard Lewis, Marvin Lynn, Jeff Philips, Richard Reed, Jay Rehak, George Rhodes, Aaron Robinson, Preston Robinson, David Stovall, Aaron Temple, Carey Lee Temple, Eric Temple, Eugene Temple, Jerry Temple.

I am grateful for my North Carolina family: Dasan Ahanu, Crystal Apple, Kim Arrington, Angel Banks, Anne Bryan, Joseph "Church da Poet", Warren Christian, Kevin Claybren, Eldrin Deas, Heather Coffey Eversley, Yolanda Gardner, Domonique Garland, Will Jackson, Ashley Leak, Margarita Machado-Casas, Thomas Patterson, Heather Rasberry Raper, Melissa Rasberry, Angela Ray, Marta Sanchez, Callie Womble, Raena Boston Yancy.

I am grateful for my colleagues, partners, mentors, and youth of Donoghue Charter; the School of Education Culture, Curriculum, Change family and Dean Bill McDiarmid; the Chapel Hill Writing Center and Kim Abels; Education Pioneers and Ann Levy Walden; Northeastern University, CPS family, and Mya Mangawang.

I am grateful for Michel Lokhorst, Jolanda Karada, and the Sense Publishers team who worked to bring this book to complete fruition.

I am grateful for each mother who spent time with me for this project and beyond. I am grateful that each one of you trusted me and continued to say, "whatever you need…" Thank you for sharing your stories, your children, your pedagogy, your friendship.

I am grateful for every village that has raised me.

ABOUT THE COVER ARTIST

Joyce Owens (Howard University, BFA; Yale University, MFA) is a painter, sculptor, curator, juror, author, consultant, wife, and mother of two sons. A native of Philadelphia, Owens has resided in Chicago for nearly 20 years. A tenured professor at Chicago State University, her award-winning art has been selected as illustrations for events, books, and exhibited on four continents including at NATA in Brussels and the African Mission in Addis Ababa, Ethiopia.

Of *Because I Am Free,* she writes: "Looking at our shared history that started in Africa, and forward to a time when wars end and we all live in peace, able to accept our differences and exist side by side." This work is currently housed in the Preston Jackson Collection.

CHAPTER 1

INTRODUCTION

The quality of light by which we scrutinize our lives has direct bearing upon the product which we live, and upon the changes which we hope to bring about through those lives. It is within this light that we form those ideas by which we pursue our magic and make it realized.
                                                – Audre Lorde, "Poetry Is not a Luxury," 1977

We Can Speak for Ourselves is an ethnographic project in which I examine Black[1] women's experiences as mothers in urban communities of Chicago. This book builds on the work of feminist and critical race scholars who have shared the ethnographic and anthropological narratives that highlight the activism of Black women during Freedom Summer (Moore, 2009; Clemons, 2014), the lived experiences of Black women ranging across the Deep South, and Northern "Black Belts" (Hurston, 1935/1995; Clark Hine & Thompson, 1999; Morrison, 2008), and the knowledge production of Black women across identities (Generett & Jeffries, 2003; Moore, 2005; Alexander Craft, McNeal, Mwangola, & Zabriskie, 2007) – to examine the race, class, and gender politics at play during this historical moment.

RESEARCH PROBLEM

Since early 2011, an onslaught of reports, campaigns, images, and legal cases have culminated in a relentless pursuit to shape public and private perceptions of Black women's and mothers' identities: the *Life Always* campaign that proclaimed "the most dangerous place for an African American is in the womb" (February 2011); the *Psychology Today* report that maligned Black women's beauty and intellect (May 2011); the Fox comedy-drama *Glee* (2009) which broadcast derisive images of an angry Black mother to a national viewership of seven million people (a Google search for "angry glee mom" currently yields an image for a dark-skinned Black woman with puffed cheeks and bulging eyes holding a hand-written poster over her own head which states in large, bold lettering "ANGRY"); and the arrests of Kelly Williams Bolar, Tonya McDowell, and Raquel Nelson are a poignant sampling.[2] A space has opened "to begin taking seriously the idea that black women's experiences act as a democratic litmus test for the nation" (Harris-Perry, 2011, p. 16).

I am discussing perceptions that not only come through the everyday consumption of controlling images that help "justify U.S. Black women's oppression" (Hill-Collins, 2004a, p. 47), but also from dominant discourses of parent involvement, mothering, and government literature. These discourses that provide a monolithic view of middle-class norms, or paint a deficit model of working class and mothers as the primary parent, are taken-for-granted representations that can readily feed public perceptions which are crippling for Black mothers. These representations essentially place Black mothers into two camps: those who are disciplined to agree with the schooling system and those who require special intervention. Furthermore, images of Black mothers, particularly those in poverty, have been shaped by "paradoxical belief systems" (Cooper & McCoy, 2009, p. 46). When Black mothers are not depicted as poor, lazy, combative, apathetic, emasculating "women who head culturally deficient families" (Hill-Collins, 1990/2009; Hancock, 2004; Cooper & McCoy, 2009), they are mythical strong Black women (Giddings, 1984; Hill-Collins, 1990/2009) who are revered amongst the masses, both Black and White, for rising above their perpetual circumstances. Therefore, this work is an intervention of self-representation that provides a counternarrative from Black mothers.

POSITIONALITY

One of the initial questions of this project was "how often do we interact with Black mothers and in what context?" As a Black woman, my response is very personal and intimate; this is the only mother I've known. I remember learning my alphabet, vocabulary words, poems, and speeches with her through songs she would sing during our morning car rides. I remember boarding the big yellow bus at the end of my school day, only to be later deposited at her school for more lessons; my mother was a middle-school Social Studies teacher in a major urban city we called home. The climate of my life in the mid 1980's was full of promise, mobility, and "Black on Black Love"[3] our community celebrated the first – and only – Black mayor[4] all four years of his tenure; and most families I interacted with were Black and middle class, which didn't make *The Cosbys*[5] seem so abstract.

The women of these families shared the responsibility of raising me. These mothers met with one another to see if their respective homes were suitable for us to play; that is if they hadn't already interacted during PTA meetings or school assemblies. Our mothers openly discussed our value systems and our plans for achievement. We were encouraged to participate in everything from karate, classical piano, Young Engineers Club and the apex of all was *school*. The first question almost anyone asked me was, "how are your grades?" which was followed by, "what high school are you thinking about... what college?" This community of women were multi-generation educators, members of HBCU and Ivy League legacies or returning to school for job promotions. They are mothers of chief executive officers and small business owners, astronauts, Broadway thespians, mothers, and educators. We have been raised by a village, and this is very apparent in my life; I was an honor student, high school debutante // and following the death of my father, a college dropout, minimum wage barista // turned self-published poet, doctor. This trajectory does not occur in isolation, and there were certainly seasons where I was as gifted as I was troubled. But there was a village.

Exchanging stories as an adult, I learned of a woman who simply changed religions to ensure that both her children *and* grandchildren attended the best school in the neighborhood – which happened to be Catholic. And another mother, whose child came home one day, totally bewildered, asking if he is Black. (Yes, he is.) She immediately pulled him from this affluent, predominately White, suburban school he attended and transferred him to a selective-enrollment, predominately Black school in the middle of the city. Dr. Mahalia Ann Hines, a child daycare provider, Chicago Public School (CPS) teacher, principal, and mother of Common (a Grammy-winning, Hollywood actor, AIDS activist, and children's philanthropist, born and raised on the South Side of Chicago), recalls her efforts and the legacy she inherited: "Even though my mother always stressed education and pushed me to succeed, I also received a separate education in how to survive… You have a door closed in your face? You have to learn how to pick the lock or maybe just knock it off the hinges" (Common & Bradley, 2011, p. 14). This perspective mirrors countless narratives of Black women, shadowed by the dominant discourse, all of which clearly state: we do not have to be told how to raise our children. Our mothers and grandmothers had a 'we will do whatever it takes' attitude when it came to our care and education. These are parts of a legacy that thread and interlock our history as Africans in America.

SIGNIFICANCE AND AUDIENCE

I consciously share the lived experiences of mothers transmitting love to their children – to "poignantly express the need [as an] African-American woman to honor our mothers' sacrifices by developing self-defined analyses of Black motherhood" (Hill-Collins, 1990/2009, p. 187). The institution of womanhood/mothering is where I was taught discipline, deference, reciprocity, and service. These lessons have weaved themselves through every narrative I write. These narratives are seamless. These narratives are invaluable. Yet in the world of rigorous, highly-vetted research, these narratives are deemed invalid. In *The Ethnocentric Basis of Social Science Knowledge Production,* John Stanfield (1985) asserts narratives, rather, "this provocative literature tends to be too impressionistic to be of much long-term value. Its shallow substance, promises, and conclusions can be attributed to at least three problems" (p. 387). It is too emotional, lacks intellectual skills, and most importantly, lacks institutional support. While I address the latter in the "Openings" chapter of this book, I am grateful for the introduction of Patricia Hill-Collins to my academic body of knowledge. This enabled me to better understand the social and intellectual value of both the narratives and the actions of Black mothers.

Before reading *The Social Construction of Black Feminist Thought* (Hill-Collins, 1989/1995), I never critically thought of all these women I interacted with as a network of activists. They were simply doing what was necessary for us as children and our community as a whole; this is the work of othermothers – a role as old as our time in America, rooted in our African ways of knowing (Hill-Collins, 1990/2009). Othermothers are women who are concerned with the holistic care of their children,

3

whether by birth or community right.[6] These women are my first examples of field workers and their lived experiences, which they shared with me day in and day out, have always been concrete criterion for meaning (Hill-Collins, 1990/2009). Upon reading the work of sisterscholars who move through and beyond academic spaces to articulate their work, whether through blogs, popular magazines, or community-based workshops, I increasingly found myself drawn to the likes of Michele Berger, Kristal Moore Clemons, and Robin Boylorn (2013a) who shares:

> Our uninterrogated investment in naming ourselves and creating opportunities from our circumstances was fiercely feminist, but we just called it "getting by." I was surrounded by reluctant feminists whose involvement in my success, happiness, and well-being was informed by an understanding that didn't require academic degrees. We were black women in a world that was as sexist as it was racist. And all we had was each other. (p. 73)

I know mothers to be fiercely protective and strict disciplinarians in their children's lives and this is certainly not limited to Black mothers. Many television shows and movies depict mothers of diverse races/ethnicities as meddlesome, opinionated, and controlling – all in the name of 'knowing what is best,' regardless of their children's age, geographic location or marital status. However, this lens does shift when considering the Black mother and understanding this distinction is crucial in how we interact with both her and her children. From a historical perspective, she is raising her children to enter, perform, and gain success within systems that have been designed to destroy them psychologically, intellectually, economically, and physically. Her teachings of survival and cultivation are not translated and characterized as that of a "Tiger Mom."[7] Instead, she has been publically (mis)translated into quick head snaps and sharp tongues. Her presence and physical appearances are not made just for comedies and heartfelt dramas; the Black Mother has been the target of government policies, law, and education literature loaded with the oppressive caricatures of submission, sexuality, and defiance.[8] The same systems for which the Black mother prepares her child appear to work at the root by leveling attacks against her. In as much as this project is a tool of affirmation for the work we do as Black mothers, it is also a teaching tool for those who only interact with us through a white patriarchal lens – particularly those we must forge collaborative relationships with in raising our children.

CONTEXT

The common factor for the women in this project is Chicago – where they were either raised or are currently raising children enrolled in the same elementary school. Chicago is a city rich with a strong, interminable history in union organizing, urban education (within a mayor-controlled school system – as he selects its Chief Executive Officer),[9] and historically segregated housing and gentrification projects, which in large parts determine the schooling experiences and sociocultural messages that are cycled for generations. Chicago Public Schools is the third largest school system in the United States. Enrollment for the 2014 fiscal year was over 400,000 students across 664 schools (516 are traditional) (Chicago Public Schools, 2014a) with an operating budget of 4.9 billion (Chicago Public Schools, 2014b) including the CEO salary of approximately $250,000 (Byrne, 2012).

In February 2012, the current city mayor – Rahm Emanuel – made the decision to close 17 underperforming elementary and secondary schools with a plan to redistribute resources, teachers, and of course, our children. In September 2012, CPS teachers and workers engaged a 19-day strike – for the first time in 25 years – partly to oppose the continuation of such efforts (Myerson, 2012). However, six months later CPS officials proposed another 54 school closures. The *Chicago-Sun Times* cover story for March 7, 2013, read: "'NOT FAIR' Though 41.7 percent of CPS students are African-American, 88 percent of students at schools targeted for closing are black." Additionally, since Arne Duncan ended his eight-year tenure as CPS CEO to accept the Secretary of Education position in 2009, the leadership has turned over five times and of the seven people to assume this office only two (Jean-Claude Brizard and Barbara Byrd-Bennett) had professional experience in Education.[10] Collectively, these moves have been characterized as education apartheid because it disproportionally affects Black families and teachers (Fitzpatrick & Golab, 2013; Rossi, 2012).

Decisions such as these precipitated into the brutal death of Derrion Albert (1993–2009), which was captured on YouTube and summoned Duncan to declare the tragedy a "wake up call for the country" (Martinez, 2009b). In this case, as mandated by the recent regulations of CPS, a low-performing high school was closed and its students were squeezed into another in the same neighborhood – doubling class sizes and mixing histories of long-standing untreated violence and hostility. It was the proverbial recipe for disaster. Annette Holt, mother of Blair Holt, who was killed two years prior noted, "someone said [Derrion] was in the wrong place at the wrong time. No, he wasn't. He was in the right place. He was coming from school" (Martinez, 2009a). These experiences are what I hear, feel, see, and know when parents say, "CPS is not an option." Additionally, we know the war is not just amongst our children, but this war includes the mayor, the Local School Councils, the Teachers' Union, the school faculties/staff, administrators on Clark Street,[11] community organizations, and every family concerned with the well-being of their children when they send them to school.

SSCES AND THE JOURNEY OF THIS PROJECT

The summer of 2010, I was granted the opportunity to work in Chicago for a 10-week education fellowship. I was assigned to South Side Charter Elementary School (SSCES)[12] which services students grades K-8. Several SSCES parents remarked that the neighborhood public school was "not an option" as many were closed or closing due to low-performance. The expressed goal for many of these parents is to graduate their children into one of the highly competitive, selective-enrollment schools in the city.[13]

SSCES boasts an art-infused program that attracts many families from across the city in addition to the open-enrollment policy; therefore, there is a waiting list for each grade. During my time there, I fielded many calls from parents and others who simply showed up to the main office, desperate to enroll their child stating:

- *"They labeled my child a behavior problem at his old school but when he got to the new school and started making A's and B's again the violence after school was too much so I need him to be here."*
- *"I don't care how long the waiting list is, my child belongs here. God will make a way."*
- *"I will go to hell and back for my children. I will hold myself and this school accountable for their success."*

As one parent was leaving with her new enrollment package, her kindergarten son turned around to me and said, *"I'm going to wear a cap and gown from this school,"* smiled and ran out of the door. It is then heartbreaking to know that between the lottery and residential redistricting that there is not always a "choice."

From my understanding, before most parents saw a curriculum or met their first teacher, they were invested in SSCES, certainly as one of the major stakeholders[14] in the school. I'd worked in the Chicago school system for nearly 10 years and had a strong working relationship with parents. This is why I was selected for this project – to develop a Parent University,[15] which is a theoretical space for parents to foster involvement with their children's school and their overall learning experience. The events and incentives I developed would incorporate school parents, various city resources, as well as the faculty and staff. During my first week, the school's Family Coordinator – Carolyn – previously organized with several parents to host a meeting for other parents in the school to create a plan of action for the upcoming school year. This meeting was a major springboard for both the Parent University and the parent involvement program, The Beacons, which at one time boasted a roster of 50 parents.

The meeting was to be the first of several which began approximately at 9AM and would run through the afternoon. It was planned for three different "drop in" stages: the first hour was scheduled for parents who identified as "very satisfied" with the school; the second hour was scheduled for parents who were on-the-fence so to speak; the latter hour was for parents who were dissatisfied and wanted to voice major concerns they were having with the school. The school faculty and administrators were not present for this meeting because it was made clear that Carolyn and the parents needed this space to be as transparent as possible. Even though the meeting was taking place in the school building, it was clear that no one would feel comfortable speaking "too freely" if *they* were there. Because the school was fairly new (less than 10 years old) – and the principal had just assumed her position that academic year, everyone wanted to create dialogue with as much honest feedback as possible from every possible perspective to effectively meet the holistic needs of the SSCES community.

Only about five of us had gathered in a resource classroom for our first Saturday morning meeting when Deja arrived. Upon seeing her, I thought she was one of those parents who made you want to walk in the opposite direction upon approach – the "pound of flesh" parent who was there only to point fingers. She was out of breath when she reached the doorway, and her unkempt hair was barely tucked under a baseball cap. She sat her McDonald's bag at the meeting table and began to complain about her ongoing job search. I looked away dismissing the conversation she was pressing with other parents who were obviously more familiar with her. As the meeting picked up, these parents began a fervent exchange about the goals for their children. The general nature of this meeting was to discuss how to extend and build more resources to develop a fertile network for all of the parents and the school. I took copious notes of their responses to questions such as "what makes a successful school?" and "what can we do now?" Over and over, I heard the words, *consistency, accountability, communication, trust,* and *transparency*. It is important for me to note that only the first stage of parents were present – the "very satisfied." However, Deja kept my attention. What took me back the most was when she pulled reports and articles from her bag addressing teacher retention, student success, and so forth. She brought literature to underscore current challenges in the classroom, the school-at-large, and how the parents present could organize themselves to be more involved. Her goals for this meeting aligned with the budding organization's guiding principles. With three biological children and othermother to her sister's children, she has a major stake in the school.

I felt ashamed for how I initially judged her. I thought she was there only to complain. I thought she was there to tell us how bad the teachers were. I thought she was there to explain to us that her child wasn't a problem; the school was. I recognized her as the archetypal Black mother for whom many pre-service teachers are warned. I translated her rushed appearance and relaxed tongue as unmotivated and confrontational. As a "good researcher" and community member, I didn't even realize I was coming in with such a strong bias. Additionally, the initial framing of this program – to teach and incentivize the parents – did not allow me to actually see her and ultimately, them.

Before developing the University, my textbook research offered fill-in charts and tables of 'Homework Time,' 'Classroom Duties,' and laundry lists of things parents can do to promote academic success. I found everything in my research on 'getting parents more involved,' except the actual perspectives and voices of the parents, which made my time with the mothers in this community all the more transformative. I'd taken the words of Umoja Student Development Corporation Director Lila Leff to heart: "no one shows up for programs, they show up for relationships" (personal communication, 2010). I'd been 'beating the street' by going to meetings at the alderwoman's office, several neighborhood restaurants, professional development workshops and felt the hope of parents when I received their new-student enrollment packets. In 10 weeks, I was able to co-create a year-long calendar of events for the parents; however, the University and Beacons were disbanded after the first three months. Because of the energy I experienced with those mothers, I was heartbroken and felt as though I had failed them in some way. I immediately wanted to know what happened; I constructed research questions from a place of hurt and was ready to point all of my fingers. In many ways, this project initially sought to answer a problem I thought I already understood. As I began to engage with the mothers, I realized that I still had much to learn about *them*. To focus on the issues of the school would not only position the administration as an enemy, which was not my intent – nor was it true, but would also further marginalize these mothers' needs and goals for their children, which had been my primary focus. I slowly realized that the nuanced perspectives of these mothers was rich in its own right and the school was not the point of departure, but the mothers could stand and speak on their own.

RESEARCH QUESTIONS

So what is the trade-off for bringing Black mothers to the Ivory Tower? They've been to this stage before, as crackheads, welfare queens, mammies, and castrating matriarchs (Davis, 1993). It is then important for me to examine the ways in which these womenn are positioned across categories of gender, race, and class, as well as categories of their nomination. My research fails if space is not created for *them* to ask questions and to use this project to their own ends.

We (my participants and self) are writing Black mothers – and ultimately Black women – into the literature via our lived experiences. I define "we" through the lens of Sofia Villenas (1996) who writes from the perspective of the colonized and the colonizer, challenging researchers of color to control their multiplicity of identity, history of complicity and mark their own points of marginalization. This is a space where we shift the light to "pursue our magic and make it realized" (Lorde, 1977/2007, p. 36). Critical ethnographer and mother Renée Alexander Craft notes, "Black women have not been waiting to be called. We are simply inviting people into a conversation that is already taking place. We are – and have been – on the front lines" (personal communication, 2011). Black women's work has pushed itself through various disciplines dating to the early 19th century. The articulations of Sojourner Truth (b. 1797), Maria Miller Stewart (b. 1803), Anna Julia Cooper (b. 1859) – who were in their respective fields before and alongside Elizabeth Cady Stanton and W.E.B. DuBois[16] – are critical intersectional contributions, which have too long existed in shadows. As Barbara Omolade (1994) wrote of being "a product of an intellectual tradition which until twenty-five years ago did not exist within the academy" (p. ix), the excavation of Black women and mother's theory and praxis have been documented through the enslavement of Africans in the U.S. (i.e., the African Holocaust or the Maafa)[17] to our current Hip Hop/technology generation in major anthologies, legal briefs, special edition journals, fiction, and song (see *Tomorrow's Tomorrow* [Ladner, 1971]; *Ain't I a Woman* [hooks, 1981]; *All the Women are White, All the Blacks are Men, But Some of Us are Brave* [Hull, Bell-Scott,

& Smith, 1982]; *In Search of Our Mothers' Gardens* [Walker, 1983]; *When and Where I Enter* [Giddings, 1984]; *Their Highest Potential* [Walker, 1996]; *How Long, How Long* [Robnett, 2000]; *Labor of Love, Labor of Sorrow* [Jones, 2009]). This work simply and directly asks, "are you paying attention?"

The goals of this work are to further a dialogue that questions how Black women come to understand their relationship to education, the role of schooling, and to contribute to the growing literature and practices of motherwork from their homes and respective communities. I am particularly interested in further exploration of how Black women develop ways of knowing regarding teaching, activism, race, and womanhood. I will also give consideration to how these women's narratives can potentially impact in-school relationships. This work, which will offer a rich perspective of Black women as mothers, othermothers, and daughters in 21st century Chicago, has four central questions:

1. What perspectives are present in the narratives of Black mothers?
2. What does it look like when Black mothers advocate?
3. How do these Black mothers' understandings of parent involvement speak to the dominant discourse?
4. How are the narratives of Black women different/similar to one another?

METHODS

My fieldwork for this project began in the summer of 2010. To examine the ideologies and impact of the women I interacted with, I sent a recruitment notification to ten women who were active members of The Beacons. Five of them agreed to be interviewed.[18] All of them had served in key positions of the organization. A qualitative methods approach was employed in two rounds of interviews with the women: the first round focused on their schooling experiences and decisions they make on behalf of their children. The second round was based on the Mothering framework (Hill-Collins, 2004a), which specifically asked the participants to explore and name the nuances of intergenerational and intercommunal relationships and support systems; family traditions and expectations; agency and activism. The interviews were coded and analyzed as narratives and coupled with the reflexive journaling of my participation as both a researcher and an othermother. Black feminist epistemology is the theoretical framework that has directed this project, fieldwork and interpretation of findings.

BLACK FEMINIST THEORY

Black feminist theory (BFT) has it roots in standpoint theory: a feminist materialism that enables us to expand the Marxian critique of capitalism to include all of human activity, especially the activity of women (Hill-Collins, 1990/2009; Hartsock, 1983). According to Black feminist theorist and activist Pearl Cleage (1994), feminism is

9

"the belief that women are full human beings capable of participation and leadership in the full range of human activities – intellectual, political, social, sexual, spiritual, and economic" (p. 28). In reference to her 2000 work *Feminism Is for Everybody*, bell hooks states "feminism is a movement to end patriarchy, to end sexism and sexist domination, and oppression. It's not difficult," also having noting "let us remember – if you take nothing else with you tonight – patriarchy has no gender" (hooks, 2014). Employing Black feminism provides support for examining how issues affecting Black women in the U.S. are part of women's global emancipation struggles (Davis, 1989/1990; Hill-Collins, 1990/2009; Moore, 2009). Therefore, BFT is critical to this project as it values the intellectual and active contributions of Black women and Black mothers. I write this as a "daughter of feminist privilege" (Morgan, 1999, p. 59).

For a Black woman to claim a feminist identity in light of the housewives' concerns' explored in Betty Friedan's *The Feminine Mystique* (1963) is a strategic, revolutionary shift of lens to explore the issues that have been affecting *masses* of women, such as economic survival and racial discrimination (hooks, 1981). Black feminist Linda La Rue (1970/1995) ardently asserts that "attempt[s] to analogize black oppression with the plight of the American white woman has the validity of comparing the neck of a hanging man with the hands of an amateur mountain climber with rope burns" (p. 164). This community urgency to break from the patriarchal press of White 'sisters' *and* Black 'brothers,' which is not set in direct opposition to either, seeks to acknowledge the entire body of feminist praxis – not just that done in "waves."[19] Whereas Friedan (1963) grew up never knowing a woman "who used her mind, played her own part in the world, and also loved, and had children" (p. 68), Black feminism affirms a lineage that concretely chronicles Black women's steadfast intellectual, spiritual, and physical participation in *every* facet of the Black liberation struggle. I acknowledge that while the term feminism was created in an academic space, *Black feminism* (Smith, 1983/2000; Boylorn, 2013c) was created in our proverbial kitchens and I do not shed this epistemological standpoint – or tool – when designing and conducting research (Grande, 2004).

Black women and mothers' identity. The theme of identity is a tightrope walk for mothers to plant positive self-affirmations for their children in the midst of protecting them from a society where they are systematically cut down. While in the womb, Black children are inherently subjected to the persistent and controlling images of their mothers. Challenging these images is a staple of Black feminism. Hill-Collins writes, "portraying African-American women as stereotypical mammies, matriarchs, welfare recipients, and hot mamas helps justify U.S. Black women's oppression" (2004a, p. 47). Images of Black motherhood align with stereotypes of Jezebel, Sapphire, and Mammy – the accepted depictions of women as chattel that have sustained American post-colonial behaviors. While all of these images are deliberately antithetical to the beauty and grace of the Victorian White woman, they have distinct roles.

The Jezebel is a sexual deviate and breeder of the enslavers' children. Her sexual relationships with the men of the plantation are never viewed as rape – for she is a temptress. Sapphire is rough, domineering, and emasculating – your all-purpose belligerent black bitch. Mammy, in contrast to both, is asexual, afeminine, virtuous, and conformable. She operates the inner-workings of *two* households (the enslaver's and her own) and tends to the enslaver's children with great care. In reality, many Mammies were not only the *sexual* property of the enslaver, but breast fed the children of the house – assuming responsibilities of the 'delicate' White mistress. Such work denied her the opportunity to care wholly for her own children. Dominant society regards Mammy as close to traditional womanhood as a Black woman can come: pious, pure, submissive, and domestic (read: non-threatening). Crucial to these identities is the intersection of mother – more accurately noted as breeding – a necessary function of both science and capitalism to maintain the system of slavery after the import of Africans legally ended (Roberts, 1997; Jenkins Schwartz, 2010).

Of the three images, Mammy is the most persistent. An advertisement for a 1910 vocational school in Athens, Georgia stated its mission to "train the Negro in the arts and industries that made the 'old Black Mammy' valuable and worthy… where men and women learn to work, how to work, and to love their work" (Roberts, 1997, p. 13). Her caricature – an overweight, jubilant, and 'Crayola' black woman, was produced as early as 1889 with the manufacture of Aunt Jemima pancakes – which is still an active image in this millennium – and was converted into a celluloid image by Hollywood productions in 1915 (Dates & Barlow, 1993). This is the long-standing, upright image to which a Black mother should aspire, and any variation deems her sub-deviant (Hill-Collins, 1990/2009, 2004a; Austin, 2003). It is here we locate the contemporary creation and perpetuation of Welfare Queen (WQ),[20] Crack Mother (CM), and Teenage-Baby-Mama (TBM; i.e., lazy, reckless, and promiscuous), of which any Black woman can be a combination of the two or three.

It is largely assumed that Black mothers purposely have children to create a larger government-issued income (i.e., WQ) which feeds into their lack of motivation and intelligence. Now, passed down through genetics and practice is an increased rate of unwed mothers.

> There is a widespread belief that poor black women who raise children alone in socially and economically isolated enclaves encourage teenage pregnancy by example, subsidize it through informal friendship and extended family networks, and justify it by prizing motherhood, devaluing marriage, and condoning welfare dependency. (Austin, 2003, p. 303)

While there has been a dramatic increase among unwed White mothers since 1965 (Roberts, 1997), it is persistently "viewed as a Black cultural trait that is creeping into white homes… White childbearing is generally heralded as a beneficial activity; it brings personal joy and allows the nation to flourish. Black reproduction, on the other hand, is treated as a form of *degeneracy*" (p. 9).

11

The media has turned its proverbial blade into this fact: *Precious* an Oscar-nominated film presents a sexually and physically violent woman as the lead character's mother, whom Patricia Hill-Collins (2004b) identifies as the stereotypical Bad Black Mother (BBM). Not only is this BBM portrayal honored with the Best Supporting Actress award, the movie fires away scene after scene without critical examination to present Precious – a young, unwed, obese, illiterate, Black girl has contracted HIV after being raped by her father and subsequently birthed a special needs daughter. In the same season, Bristol Palin, daughter of GOP Vice Presidential candidate Sarah Palin, was brought to light as a courageous, teenage, unwed, mother asserting her pro-choice rights and has since reportedly garnered over a quarter of a million dollars as a spokesperson for young adult unplanned pregnancies. Bristol Palin's child was never called *illegitimate.* Nevertheless, both images were celebrated for their respective reasons. The former is posed to remind us that Black unwed mothers are "carrying on like modern-day Jezebels when they should be acting like good revisionist Mammies" (Austin, 2003, p. 305).

These psychological identities can only appear less threatening when compared to the physical detriment and criminalization of Black mothers who are crack users. This drug was introduced to the Black community in the early 1980s and has stimulated the rapid and rabid effect of community deterioration in 10 years almost akin to 100 years of the Maafa. It is not easy to argue against the issue that Black mothers and injurious drug use are a concern for child rights at best and a form of genocide at worst; however, to use child rights as a scapegoat to punish poor, Black women should be considered proportionately vile. It is not just that these women are drug users, but *crack* users and of special note are the legal manipulations which have ensured the prosecution of Black women and their reproductive rights, often deterring addicts from counseling and treatment services due to the sure threat of incarceration or determinate division from their other children (Roberts, 1997, p. 167). Targeting this form of drug use – as opposed to alcohol and/or prescription drugs, which also affect fetuses at markedly high rates – exposes the issue of class and race. This is reminiscent of Oscar Lewis' work on the "culture of poverty" (which has been rebottled and sold to pre-service teachers and professional development seminars via Ruby Payne) that lists cultural traits of the poor to be "lazy, fatalistic, hedonistic, violent, distrustful, people living in common law unions, as well as in dysfunctional, female-centered, authoritarian families who are chronically unemployed and rarely participate in local civic activities, vote, or trust the police and political leaders" (Foley, 1997, p. 115). This sweeping indictment of "the poor" makes it easy to launch "War." It appears that the aim is to punish and prohibit the reproductive rights of Black women who have not made the best of their precarious situations while keeping a tight fist on treatment and rehabilitation, which should also be in the best interest of the child's health, not just the jail sentences and abductions.

These images and issues illuminate the critical need for Black feminism as it asserts that the work of Black mothers has been about more than "dishpan hands" (La Rue, 1970/1995, p. 164). The historical characterizations of the Black woman position her as combative, apathetic, and emasculating, especially in her home. The reality is that home leadership is narrowly defined by who earns the (larger) paycheck, deemphasizing that major family decisions are often a *shared* responsibility despite financial income. In fact, Black mothers have often been penalized by the government for securing legal relationships with their partners, thereby bloating the statistics of single and female-headed households. Additionally, Black mothers have actually been accused of suffocating their sons and daughters while they have worked beyond capacity to protect their children from a society that has brutally and fatally penalized young Black boys and girls for asserting their manhood or demoralizing their sexuality, without the protection or service of the law. While care and personal responsibility have been staples of motherhood, it is crucial to view the work of Black mothers in a context that is situated in their lived experiences and through personal dialogue (Hill-Collins, 1990/2009).

The most prominent lenses created to examine the lives of Black women are Black Feminist Thought (BFT; Hill-Collins, 1990/2009); Intersectionality (Crenshaw, 1989); Womanism (Walker, 1983); and Critical Race Feminism (Wing, 1997/2003). The potency of these lenses is far greater than their splitting hairs; each lens projects Black women as agents of change and creators of knowledge. This potency is evidenced by the overlapping works of Black women, which blur discipline lines toward a collective experience. However, for the frame of this project, BFT is most beneficial to define and explore the varied positions and perspectives of Black mothers. BFT is connected to a lineage that examines the work of Black women through their enslavement in this country, to suffrage, to civil rights, and family rights, which are important as the *work* life of Black women predates the feminist movement that houses much of the literature on motherhood. The work of Patricia Hill-Collins (1990/2009) is most poignant as she posits four tenets of BFT that are central to both theory and method: (1) lived experience is the concrete criterion for meaning (2) the use of dialogue to assess knowledge claims (3) the ethic of caring (4) the ethic of personal responsibility. All of these tenets directly inform the work of Black mothers.

MOTHERWORK

Patricia Hill-Collins (1990/2009) posits that there has been a collective reluctance of U.S. Black women to contribute to critical analyses of Black motherhood because of the persistent discourse posed by feminism, with limited effectiveness due to "the combination of its perceived Whiteness and antifamily politics" (p. 190). This is why it is critical to understand the varied discourse on motherhood. Early feminist work – particularly through the 1980's – held a limited critique of motherhood that ignored complexities of race and class and organized family life into two spheres: public and private, i.e., separation of work and home.

Motherwork (Hill-Collins, 2004a) is then presented as a challenge to these separate spheres. This framework is grounded in Black women's agency and concerned with social problems such as: child care for U.S. Black mothers; education opportunities for Black children; the prison pipeline for Black men; and the disproportionate numbers of Black children in foster care. Hill-Collins uses the term motherwork which "can be done on behalf of one's own biological children, or for the children of one's own racial ethnic community, or to preserve the earth for those children who are yet unborn" (2004a, p. 48). In earlier writing, she explores five types of motherwork. This includes:

- *Women Centered Networks (WCN)* are described as a community of mothers, grandmothers, sisters, aunts, cousins, [or neighbors] responsible for taking care of the children. Because of the historical value of WCN, many of these women grow to gain "a reputation for never turning away a needy child" (Hill-Collins, 1990/2009, p. 198).
- *Mothers and Daughters* describes the ways mothers communicate love in an environment that calls for their protection and survival.
- *Community Othermothers and Political Activism* describes "mothering of the mind" which demands socially responsible uses of education.
- *Motherhood as a Symbol of Power* explores issues of class, the dumbing down of Black women's work and the work of community women who are "nameless in scholarly texts, yet everyone in their neighborhoods knows their names" (1990/2009, p. 208).
- *The View from the Inside* describes mothering as a "fundamentally contradictory institution" (1990/2009, p. 211) and shares the narratives of Black mothers.

FORWARD

This chapter has provided an introduction to the research problem, significance, the journey of the project, methods, and epistemology. Chapter 2 explores the dominant discourses that focus on Black mothers. I specifically discuss the literature from scientific research; government reform; motherhood and parent involvement; popular media; and briefly introduce the perspectives of the women who have participated in this project as a means of "speaking back" (G. Noblit, personal communication, 2012). Chapter 3 provides the methods for this ethnographic project. In Chapter 4, the women speak. Chapter 5 provides an interpretation and analysis of the narratives according to four themes and reflexive journaling. Chapter 6 will conclude by addressing the implications of these Black mothers' lived and shared experiences. An Epilogue is provided to discuss the emergence of violence that has occurred since this project formally concluded in early 2012. Current issues are explored with respect to a historical lens; social media as a literature source; maps for further research; and challenges to multiple audiences.

NOTES

1 I maintain the use of Black as an inclusive term for those of African descent, living in the United States, who are descendants of the African Diaspora. Some references that are cited use the term African-American or People or Women of Color – especially when generally including people or women of non-White ethnic/racial groups.

2 These are explored further in Chapter 2.

3 The "Black on Black Love" campaign was a major movement in Chicago during the early 1980s. It began when Edward Gardner, founder of Soft Sheen products, placed full-page ads in major media urging community members to combat "Black on Black crime" with "Black on Black Love." I vividly remember plastering my walls with these placards and bumper stickers as a child.

4 Harold Washington (1922–1987) is the first and only Black mayor in Chicago's 175 years of governance. He served four years in this position before dying of a heart attack in his City Hall office. I recall the announcement of his death during the school day over the public announcement system; my teacher abruptly left the room completely grief-stricken.

5 The Cosby Show (1984–1992) was a prime-time, half-hour television sitcom that featured an African-American upper middle-class family of seven, largely based on the family-centered stand-up comedy routines of William H. Cosby, Jr., Ed.D. (also the show creator). Of important note are the contributions of Civil Rights Activist and Harvard (child) psychiatry professor Alvin F. Poussaint, M.D., who vetted 196 of the 197 scripts for the 8-year series.

6 In this way, I shift between the uses of mother, woman, and othermother throughout this work making the claim that everyone in discussion is concerned for the holistic care of our children and community.

7 *Battle Hymn of the Tiger Mother* (2011), by Amy Chua, a mother who examines her practices of a traditional, strict, Chinese upbringing in raising her two daughters. While the memoir in large part was intended to be a self-mocking revelation of her techniques, mixed reviews of the book regarded it as a "how-to" guide as well as an exhortation of non-Western values.

8 These are elaborated upon in Chapter 1 and 2.

9 The position of CEO was created in 1995 by Mayor Richard M. Daley, upon the decision by the Illinois State Legislature to place Chicago Public Schools under mayoral control. Paul Vallas was first appointed to this position and remained in office until 2001 (six years), preceding current US Secretary of Education Arne Duncan who held the position until 2009 (eight years).

10 Ron Huberman held the position January 2009–November 2010 (22 months) upon sudden resignation; interim CEO Terry Mazany held the position for 6 months; Jean-Claude Brizard held the position May 2011–October 2012 (17 months) upon sudden resignation; and current CEO, Barbara Byrd-Bennett held the position October 2012–June 1, 2015 having resigned after a two-month paid leave of absence amid a federal investigation into a $20.5 million no-bid contract. Jesse Ruiz assumed the interim CEO position, April 17, 2015.

11 Downtown street location of the main offices for the Chicago Board of Education.

12 All names of school, faculty, staff, parents, and programs are noted with pseudonyms.

13 It is important to note that public schools in Chicago have several categories. On the Chicago Public School website (www.cps.edu) there were 11 categories to delineate the 665 public schools in the district for the 2011–2012 school year. These categories include Neighborhood, Traditional, Optional, Contract, Military Academy, Special Education, Magnet, and Selective Enrollment. Only the first two are included when generally speaking of the dangers and failures of CPS; the others schools are deemed exceptions.

14 As current education reform measures move more toward business models of operation, the term *stakeholder* has often been employed to discuss the needs of administrators and faculty as primary consultants for school decisions. The term generally does not holistically include families and their respective communities. I intentionally use the term in this work to affirm the voices and resources of the participants.

[15] Parent Universities are designed as a theoretical space to instigate parent involvement. Ideally, the school works closely with the parents to establish a "credit system", awarding credits for various activities (e.g., lunchroom duty, class mom, trip chaperone). The parents with substantial amounts of credits are recognized at various school ceremonies and may be awarded items donated by community sponsors. The Parent University has grown popular across the country; there are some that have a physical space for parents that serve as a library and technology resource center.

[16] Foremost leaders in feminist and Black thought.

[17] The African Holocaust is an alternative term to note the enslavement of Africans in the U.S. or reference to the Trans-Atlantic Slave Trade. "Holocaust" is a term of Latin, Greek, and French languages from the mid 12th and mid 13th centuries meaning "wholly burnt" or "burnt offering." It was first recorded in 1957 in reference to the Nazi genocide of European Jews which was previously referred to as "Shoah" meaning "catastrophe." Therefore, according to its etymology, the term "holocaust" does not belong to a specific ethnic group but rather refers to a "mass slaughter of people" according to the Merriam-Webster Dictionary. In this way, scholars focused on the African Diaspora refer to this period of enslavement and disenfranchisement – roughly documented between 1525 when Portugal began exporting African bodies across the World, to the signing of the U.S. 1965 Voting Rights Act – as the African Holocaust; there are scholars who extend this period into the present with respect to the prison industry. However, because the term is so closely tied to Jewish history, anthropologist and African Studies scholar Marimba Ani (1980, 1994) refers to this period as the Maafa – a Kiswahili term meaning "great disaster." Since the late 1990's, this term has gained momentum within academic scholarship and not without controversy; however, I employ it here as a clear marker of the terrorism upon African bodies in the U.S., by not using deficit-based language such as "slavery" or to conflate it with other genocidal atrocities such as *The Holocaust.*

[18] See Appendix I.

[19] Feminist theory is historically documented in the West according to three waves. The first wave began in the nineteenth and early 20th centuries, marked by the Suffrage Movement. The second wave is associated with the Women's Liberation Movement of the 1960s. The third wave, which may run concurrently with the second, is seen as a reaction to the second wave failures. While there are a notable number of Women of Color that are included in "Third Wave" literature, collectively, these "waves" have been criticized as too static and intentionally narrow in holistically addressing the protests and progress of Black women in the US and worldwide.

[20] "Welfare Queen," a trope of Former President Ronald Reagan, was first used during his 1976 presidential campaign in reference to a woman on the South Side of Chicago (Douglas & Michaels, 2004).

CHAPTER 2

WHO SAYS WHAT ABOUT BLACK WOMEN

Review of Discourses

If Black women do not speak for themselves, other people will do it for us badly.

– Barbara Christian, 1985

Figure 1. Postcard from early 1900's. Bottom caption reads,
"Just a Nigger." Charleston, S.C.[1]

This chapter serves not only as a review of academic literature but reviews several discourses – including images (see Figure 1) – that have been instrumental in the construction of knowledge regarding Black women's bodies, psyches, and everyday lives. This review follows a historical trajectory, which begins with "Scientific Discourse" and its role in shaping "Government Discourse". The policies discussed in the latter transition the review to "Education Discourse", aligning with the "Mothering Discourse", which creates space for the primary participants of this project. To provide a contemporary understanding of Black women and mothers, a review of "Media Discourse" is provided along with current "Legal Interventions". This review concludes with an initial sampling of the participants' voices, which speak directly to the streams of discourses provided.

OUR FIRST STAGE: SCIENTIFIC DISCOURSE

Cornel West (1982/2003) asserts, "the notion that [B]lack people are human beings is a relatively new discovery in the modern West" (p. 298) (see Figure 1). While the construction of race in America is both permeable and problematic, it has had a substantial impact on law and policy; educational research and practice; and self-actualization. From a 'bottom up' perspective, this has been absolutely true – and detrimental – for Black women, particularly when we consider body rights and motherhood.

The most salient of these experiences is that of Saartjie (Sara) Baartman, or the Venus Hottentot (c.1789–1815). This Khoi/South African woman was exhibitioned throughout Europe, branded as "other", and exoticized for her large buttocks and elongated labia. While there are several historical and contemporary images of her likeness both depicting her actual body as well as caricature images, none is more piercing than the "La Belle Hottentot." One of the most popular images of Baartman is a 19th century French print depicting a London exhibition of European observers remarking on Baartman's body. There are three men in formal/uniform attire – one with a magnifying eyeglass, another with his foot in a chair as if to gain better leverage to examine her backside. In front of Baartman is a woman perched down close to her as if poised for an in-depth exploration and there is even a dog standing on his hind legs in excitement. There are three captions on the print, two of which are translated to read: "Oh! God Damn what roast beef!" and "Ah! How comical is nature."[2]

One hundred seventy years after Baartman's untimely death, cultural and literary historian Sander Gilman (1985) wrote an article that recapitulated Baartman to prominence and created a theoretical upsurge in analyses of race and gender. In *Which Bodies Matter?*, sociologist Zine Magubane (2001) makes the claim that any scholar wishing to advance an argument on gender and colonialism, gender and science, or gender and race must, it seems, quote Sander Gilman who concluded:

> The antithesis of European sexual mores and beauty is embodied in the Black, and the essential Black, the lowest rung on the great chain of being, is the Hottentot. The physical appearance of the Hottentot is, indeed, the central nineteenth-century icon for sexual difference between the European and the Black. (Gilman, 1985, p. 231)

Magubane notes this regressive direction of gender and race research which fails to take into consideration the colonial practices that in fact enslaved Baartman, paraded her as a European freakshow exhibit and dissected her body during the Romantic Period (which ironically enough, is a reaction against scientific rationalization).

Baartman is our earliest example of an intersectional approach in race-gender research, which departs from a "single-axis framework" (Crenshaw, 1989, p. 30). Whereas Black women have been regarded as either too much like women, or too much like Blacks, the heterogeneity of their experiences has been collapsed and absorbed by either group. Black *mothers* hold an even more precarious position between the two assumed binaries and are thereby regarded as too hard to define or easily erasable. It is imperative that all analyses of Black mothers take intersectionality (Crenshaw, 1989) into account to sufficiently address the particularities of their subordination and to confront the reinscription of white supremacy.

GOVERNMENT DISCOURSE

Initial analyses of Black mothers were largely conducted by men. A primary example of this work is by D. P. Moynihan, commissioned by Former President Johnson during his "War on Poverty." In the 1965 United States Labor Department report, *The Negro Family: The Case for National Action*, Moynihan narrows the problem of American society to the Negro family, specifically the mother. Citing the "Black Matriarch" as a byproduct of the Maafa which "in all its forms sharply lowered the need for achievement in slaves," he states, "the Negro community has been forced into a matriarchal structure which, because it is out of line with the rest of the American society, seriously retards the progress of the group as a whole..." Adding insult to injury, there were aspects of the report endorsed by the Black patriarchal class of the time such as Rev. Dr. Martin Luther King, Jr., Roy Wilkins, and Whitney Young (Giddings, 1984).

In *When and Where I Enter* (1984), Paula Giddings discusses the major theme of the report, which emphasizes the male's psychological and physiological need to "strut" and the reception of the report, which all but said, "just make Black men the lords of their own castles and everything will be all right" (p. 328). However, this would necessitate that Black women slow down, "become less achievement-oriented, give up much of their independence. By remaining assertive, they were ruining the family and so ruining the race" (p. 328, 329). These deficit-model analyses of Black families honed in on Black mothers and created controlling images that undergird studies that critique welfare reform, reproductive legislation, the HIV/AIDS pandemic, and education policies. These analyses were publically recycled and stood alone until the growth of modern Black feminism in the 1970's (Hill-Collins, 1990/2009).

In another critique of the "Black Matriarch," sociologist Robert Staples (1970/1981) asserts:

> the financial value set on slave children and the rewards given to successful motherhood in cash, kind, and promotion from field slave to house slave gave an especially high status to the mother, a status which the father could only enjoy if placed in a position akin to that of a stud animal, this leading to a breaking of family ties and the degradation of family life still further... The black family's desire to remain together was subordinated to the economic interests of the slave-holding class. Only the mother-child bond continually resisted the disruptive effect of economic interest.... (p. 28)

The separation of work and home are luxuries that had not been afforded the Black mother as she worked seamlessly through the enslaver's house, the fields, and her family home, from 'can see to can't see.' What can be learned from the Maafa is that Black women were forcibly brought to this country to both work *and* nurture. So whereas the female saw *promotion* through motherhood, this so-called access opened the door for both sexual exploitation and the responsibility of heading her household.

To be clear, the issue is not one of a female-headed household, it is challenging the assumptions inherent in a society that "expects and rewards male leadership," (Staples, 1970/1981, p. 31) which is constructed through a single-axis, whitestream lens. This lens informed the Moynihan Report and fostered the idea of the patriarchal need to "strut" and thereby "provide." To then identify the Black mother as a "matriarch" in this context – a label that has been defaulted to her by the cruelty of her "master" – is in fact "a classical example of what Malcolm X called making the victim the criminal" (p. 26). The challenge for Black mothers is then twofold: to work against the norm that asserts a universal search for "personal autonomy... as the human guiding quest" (p. 48) and to use her energy for the building and rebuilding of community relationships.

EDUCATION DISCOURSE

Historically, education has been understood to be one of the most powerful tools in citizenship and social mobility. Unfortunately, when Black mothers are actually named in an educational discourse, it is often through the deficit-based lens of poverty. Educational sociology literature propagated by the Moynihan Report promotes a *culture of poverty*, (Lewis, 1959) often preparing pre-service teachers to enter urban school environments in full-metal jackets, with missionary-like zeal. Charles Murray's book, *Losing Ground: American Social Policy, 1950–1980* (1984) is a significant text that reports the federal efforts and statistical analysis of education for Blacks after *Brown v. Board of Education,* reaching into wider society effects. In Part II, *Being Poor, Being Black,* Charles Murray reaffirms, "we are using blacks as our proxy for ...the poor and disadvantaged" (p. 116) and writes that many 1960s youth were functionally illiterate, without social capital and were surviving through an "explosion" of criminal activity – most notably, urban Blacks. Inserting graphs, national census data, and other research findings, the same as his co-authored work in *The Bell Curve* (1994) which sought to provide empirical evidence of the intellectual inferiority of Blacks and minorities, Murray continues in a discussion of *The Family* asserting the social detriment of illegitimate births and the fertility of Black females – particularly teenagers. It is important that teenagers are emphasized because they are often parents without a partner, limited education and resources, giving birth to moderately healthy children (using low-birth weight as an indicator of physical and mental risk problems), who are born into federal dependency. Using the next generation as a mark of progression, being poor and Black in Murray's multi-level analyses appears to provide several impenetrable arguments, where despite "however much [the poor and disadvantaged mothers] may love [their children]" (p. 129), they are statistical detriments to American society.

The poor. Murray's work is imperative in understanding how researchers and teachers, as well as the parents and children themselves, are introduced to urban schools. Ruby Payne took this lens as an opportunity to author, *A Framework: Understanding and working with students and adults from Poverty* (1995). This book, currently in its 4th edition, is marketed as a must-read for educators, policymakers, service providers (having sold nearly one million copies), and has catapulted Payne into the position of an international expert consultant on the so-called poverty mindset and education. Her career began by having informal discussions with other educators regarding her opinions on poverty and discipline. After several conversations that blossomed into formal presentations, she was encouraged to write a book on her observations. Her primary source at this time had been her husband of 22 years who experienced *situational* poverty for a brief period as a child. She then notes, that her marriage, combined with her teaching experiences, provided her with "24 years of data on poverty" (Payne, p. 2). I briefly highlight Payne's background and credentials to illuminate her influence and what passes as 'expert opinion.'

The introduction of her book lists 18 decontextualized statistical data of poverty, specifically noting the deficits of "minority children." The first chapter presents seven fictional case studies, each overrun with drug, sexual, spousal, child abuse; gang violence; welfare dependency; financial irresponsibility; illiteracy; second-language acquisition; church dependency; prostitution; incarceration; mental health concerns; single-parenting; abandonment; and the threat of homelessness. This list is exhausting; however, I write each one of the 16 deficits to provide the same sense of dramatization Payne employs to manipulate stereotypes and vilifying pictures of the "other," right down to the name choices. Her scenarios set the tone for the framework that intentionally overwhelm the reader, while they also provide a sense of relief ("whew, that's not me,") in the hopes of perhaps leveraging – not what is recognized as privilege – but an obligation to *save* these people from themselves. The work of Ruby Payne is not a simple indictment of 'poor' parenting but makes Mothers of Color the target of her emotional and unsubstantiated assumptions and assaults.

The involved. Aligned with this purpose of promoting experts' work, Joyce Epstein (2009) has created a widely-accepted framework, originally designed in 1997 and is currently in its third edition. *School, Family and Community Partnerships: Your Handbook for Action*, defines six types of opportunities for parental involvement: (1) assisting with child rearing skills, (2) school communication with the parent, (3) volunteer opportunities for the parents, (4) home-based learning for the parents, (5) involving the parents in school decision-making, and (6) involving parents in school-community collaboration. Epstein notes that this is a substantial shift from her earlier work which only emphasized basic obligations, one-way communication, school/home involvement, this framework still operates on the assumption that mothers have to be taught or *made* to be involved. These types of opportunities have a top-down approach, which posits the school, teachers, and administrators, as the primary capital holders. There are specific goals for the teachers that list "increased diversity and use of communication," and "understanding of families' backgrounds, cultures…" (p. 18). Goals for the parents are listed as "self-confidence about ability to work in school and with children, or to take steps to improve own education; awareness of child as learner; interactions with teachers and eased communications with school and teachers" (p. 18).

These opportunities for involvement are not the major point of contention of this work. Epstein lists specific goals for the benefit of the schools and the students, but does not cite opportunities for parent leadership, nor opportunities for the parents to leverage the resources they bring. The handbook includes quoted 'research' (without specific citations) stating, "affluent communities tend to have more positive family involvement, on average, *unless* schools and teachers in economically distressed communities work to build positive partnerships with their students' families" (p. 12). The expected results for teachers and parents are clear markers that Epstein writes for a community of *others* – people that must be taught appropriate school culture and parenting skills, as opposed to those who inherently know these so-called parenting rules. This framework and discourse alludes to the societal construction of moral responsibilities women have to their children, which haphazardly draws a major tension with parent involvement that is largely defined by school and state requirements (Griffin & Smith, 2005).

Redefinition of parent involvement. Parent Involvement discourse appears to ignore the narratives of Black mothers with respect to their expectations for their children, their networks of support beyond the nuclear family – generally defined as a married mother and father – and most importantly how the mothers themselves define involvement. Cooper and McCoy (2009) assert, "these maternal figures – be they biological mothers, grandmothers, or fictive kin mothers – are *all* mothers who are highly revered women [in African-American culture] seen not only as the bearer and nurturers of children, but the bearers of culture, faith, and resiliency" (p. 47). However, dominant narratives often position Black mothers as chronically impoverished subjects that need to be taught parenting (McGrath & Kuriloff, 1999). Alternatively, they are collapsed into the parent involvement discourse that "tends to favor White, middle class parents" (Fields-Smith, 2007, p. 167), rendering invisible the complexities of Black motherwork. Therefore, the issue does not squarely lie with parent involvement as much as it does with how we understand mothering.

Griffin and Smith (2005) discuss parent involvement through the lens of *mothering*, positing that the dominant discourse of parental involvement has "subordinated mothers' experiential understanding of their children to the generalities constructed

[by] child psychologists and psychiatrists, social workers and educators, and authors in the popular press and television" (p. 36). We are made to understand that mothers are not intelligent enough to speak for the development of their children and participation in their education must be mediated by 'experts.'

MOTHERING DISCOURSE

It is important to note the pivotal roles of not just parents in education, but specifically of mothers. A great deal of feminist theorizing about motherhood posed a "dichotomous split" (Hill-Collins, 2004a, p. 46), assigning gender roles that divided the family into an "archetypal white, middle-class nuclear family," (p. 46) where the men/fathers exerted power over women/mothers in both the labor market and the home. Recall this discourse organizes family life into two spheres: public and private. Patricia Hill-Collins (2004a) stresses that the public sphere emphasized economy and politics (i.e., work). The private sphere emphasized family and household responsibilities (i.e., home). Ultimately, the fathers were drawn as "workers" and mothers as "affectionate nurter[ers]" (p. 47), and the whole success of society hinged upon the adult male who achieved autonomy through this construction. Therefore, it has theoretically been the responsibility of the mother to ensure the development of the child.

However, it is not just *any* mother that could 'do the job.' This particular organization of family grants the mother the role of also ensuring "their children could reproduce the class status of their parents," (Griffin & Smith, 2005, p. 24) using the public school system as the primary vehicle. This exercise of social and cultural capital allows for the entrance of males into higher education institutions; this reproduction of class then also becomes tied to academic achievement. To create more complexity, Black mothers must make effort to emulate this class reproduction, with hairline access to class mobility; address overt and systematic racism; and adhere to pressing needs of childcare, transportation and cultural mismatching, and inadequate school environments. In this way, Black mothers must understand what are the "appropriate" behaviors for school engagement (Fields-Smith, 2007).

The National Congress of Mothers (NCM) was founded in 1897 and it was directly concerned "with schools, with further parenting influences in them, and with promoting and supporting the establishment of local parent-teacher associations (PTAs)" (Griffin & Smith, 2005, p. 23). This group had a major influence in U.S. social change until the *Red Scare*[3] of the 1920s, and their focus became limited to schooling (Ladd-Taylor, 1997; Griffin & Smith, 2005). While the NCM continued its focus upon representing local PTAs, it *excluded* the PTAs of Black women (Walker, 2000; Griffin & Smith, 2005). In 1926, Black PTAs were organized into the National Congress of Colored Parents and Teachers (NCCPT; Grant, 1998; Griffin & Smith, 2005). Their concerns not only met the needs inside of the schools but also "confronted" racism and segregation barriers (Dickson, 1998; Higginbotham, 1985; Griffin & Smith, 2005).

CONTROLLING IMAGES: MEDIA DISCOURSE

In a short span of two years, an onslaught of reports and campaigns were launched in a relentless pursuit to shape public and private perceptions of Black women's and mother's identity. An economy report issued March 9, 2010, by Insight Center for Community Economic Development stated that unmarried Black women, who are 40% of Black female population, have a median wealth of five dollars; this works to emphasize a poverty culture. Additionally, married or cohabitating Black women scarcely earn 18% of the salary of married White women (Grant, 2010). Shifting from money to health, reports have notoriously tied Black women to the rising HIV/AIDS epidemic; again in March of 2010, the Centers for Disease Control and Prevention (CDC) reported a spike in herpes – a virus that makes the body more susceptible to HIV/AIDS – and that 48% of Black women are infected[4] (Centers for Disease Control and Prevention, 2010). Noting that not only are diseases ravaging Black women's bodies, but external appearances leave much to be desired as well. Satoshi Kanazawa, a well-noted researcher and blogger with *Psychology Today,* posted the article "Why Black Women Are Less Physically Attractive Than Other Women" on May 15, 2011,[5] statistically claiming that Black women are the most unattractive, physically *and* intellectually, compared to European, Asian and Native American women. With these statistics and reports, it is not implausible to understand why Black women are not equipped to build suitable family structures and communities. The first installment of the CNN series, *Black in America: The Black Woman and Family* (2008), sparked a litany of roundtable discussions, none more shameful than, *Black Marriage Negotiations* (2010) – a viral video (reminiscent of the Shahrazad Ali 1989 manifesto, *The Blackman's Guide to Understanding the Blackwoman*), overrun with the idea that Black women cannot successfully mate with Black men, thereby dismantling the Black family. Reality television, taking its cue from the 'experts,' has banked on this spectacle with the sensationalizing of *Real Housewives of Atlanta [RHOA]* (2008), *Basketball Wives* (2010), *Love and Hip Hop* (2011), and the *Celebrity Apprentice* fiasco (fueled by one-time presidential-hopeful Donald Trump) between Nene Leakes (of *RHOA*) and Star Jones (of *The View*) in March 2011. It is clear that for every Michelle Obama, *Sesame Street* "I love my hair"[6] segment, or *Black Girls Rock* awards ceremony,[7] a feverish witch-hunt style retrenchment of the Black women's character and body has ensued.

What is most soul-piercing, is the anti-abortion campaign that has recently targeted Black women. In February 2011, a major traffic area in the SoHo neighborhood of Manhattan, New York stood a 48 foot high/14 foot high billboard featuring a 6-year old Black girl, under a caption that read: "the most dangerous place for an African American is in the womb." Another U.S. billboard of the Texas-based group, "Life Always" read: "Black Children are an Endangered Species: Too Many Abortions." Members of the same group have noted the New York message was a Black History Month commemoration (Holloway, 2011).

While these reports may state facts to raise awareness and pose calls-for-action, each and every stroke of these examples blatantly work to compose a painful portrait: We are to be reminded/told that we are broke, diseased, ugly, dumb, emasculating, unprofessional, and not just bad mothers, but murderers. These controlling images are critical strikes in how we are perceived by others. They also impact how we relate and practice with one another, which is critical in understanding that who we are as Black women is primarily shaped by women – our mothers and othermothers. As illustrated in a 1972 study by sociologist Cynthia Fuchs Epstein, the achievement of professional Black women "had little to do with advantage but a great deal to do with the attitudes of each woman's family, her sense of self-worth, the role of her mother, and her superior's perception of her" (Giddings, 1984, p. 332). Of the many lenses used to examine Black women and mothers (e.g., scientific research, government policy, media) our lived experiences are masked by stereotypes, ill-will, and self-serving benevolence. In this vein, Regina Austin (2003) notes, "Full utilization of the economic, political, and social resources that black women represent cannot depend on the demand of a society insincerely committed to an ethic of integration and equal opportunity" (p. 301).

LEGAL INTERVENTIONS

In 2011, the law publically intervened in unimaginable ways to devalue and divide the relationship between Black mothers and children. Raquel Nelson (Georgia), suffered an incredible loss when her 4-year son was struck and killed in an unmarked intersection by a motorist who had two previous hit-and-runs on his driving record, his system revealed an overdose of prescription drugs, and he was partially blind in one eye (Bluestein, 2012). After serving six months of a five-year sentence, he was released, and the county began prosecuting *Nelson* for jaywalking, reckless conduct, and second-degree vehicular manslaughter (while she does not even own a car). Held in custody, thereby separated from her two other children, facing a three-year conviction, she was convicted and sentenced to a year of probation, community service and additional *leniency* in the form a new trial. For Nelson, it was not her marital status or drugs in *her* system that made her a criminal, but her son's hand slipping from hers while crossing the street into "unsafe conditions" (Bluestein, 2012).

Earlier this same year, Kelly Williams-Bolar (Ohio) enrolled her two daughters into a highly competitive school that they were ineligible to attend because they lived in another district. After the district discovered the reported address of the girls, which was the home of their father who, in fact, did live in the district, Williams-Bolar was jailed for 10 days and sentenced to a three-year probation for falsifying documents and was required to pay $30,000 in back tuition. "The Copley-Fairlawn District, school officials said she was cheating because her daughters received a quality education without paying taxes to fund it... Those dollars need to stay home with our students" (Chang & Williams, 2011).

25

Three months later Tonya McDowell (Connecticut) was arrested for lying about her permanent address "so that her 6-year old son could attend a school outside the district of the minivan in which they were living" (Andrews, 2011). Charged with grand larceny for allegedly stealing $15,686 from Norwalk schools, she is facing the possibility of a 20-year conviction. The city mayor Richard Moccia stated, "This is an ex con, and somehow the city of Norwalk is made into the ogre in this. She has a checkered past at best" (Andrews, 2011). Perhaps Mayor Moccia, but what about our children?

The current talk in education revolves around school choice as a band-aid measure for school failure. School choice is promoted through films such as the aptly titled, *Waiting for Superman*, and the frenziedly scalable success of community and charter schools across the country. "This fits a pattern of Black parents seeking increased accountability, opportunity, choice, and voice within their children's schools, which they have done since the advent of schooling" (Cooper, 2005). However, what is the *choice* when many of the public, urban neighborhood schools look much like the prisons children will be pipelined and the alternative is to pick a number? As evidenced throughout this review, blaming the victim and criminalization of Black mothers is not at all new. Additionally, the cases of Williams-Bolar and McDowell are two contemporary examples of a rich history that dispels long-held myths that Black people – particularly low-income mothers – do not care about the education of their children; while at the same time, the 'whatever it takes' attitude is fast-becoming a punishable offense.

WE SPEAK

While the five women who participated in this project are mothers within the same school, they are not a monolithic group. They represent a range of expectations and needs developed over generations and cultural norms with significant commonalities and goals. When they were asked to define "mother", the responses included: protector, educator, nutritionist, power, champion, strong. Their responses often reflected the examples of their homes, what they longed for, or myths they work to uphold and each woman explored these definitions according to their lived experiences. They cite everyday practices without referencing one theorist or law. Much of the literature reviewed in this project was foreign to them and while some became visibly emotional when discussing the court cases and media images, each one of them was clear about her position. Sonia tells me, "I don't take it personally. My focus is more on [my son's] development." For Maya, this very clearly means planning a system of accountability and open communication between herself, her daughter, her daughter's teachers and the school administrators. "You have my cell phone, my email, my work number, but we've all spent time together, *and you know* what kind of kid she is. You have her for six hours. Do what you have to do, *then* come to me." None of these mothers claim to have read a handbook – although Maya says it would be impossible to write a completely effective one anyway. They have made the best of every resource available to them, even when it means performing so-called miracles or simply admitting, "I don't know." They do not all agree on the same choices and methods; however, they all work from a place of familiar. Maya says, "girl, as a mom – baby your gut will talk – you will know." These mothers are the first lines of defense for their children, and they consult with family, community, and school members when raising what they regard as their number one gift and responsibility.

NOTES

[1]   Image provided courtesy of Khalid el-Hakim, Black History 101 Mobile Museum.

[2]   Her remains were examined, placed on display in Musée de l'Homme (Paris) until 1974 and were not returned to her birth home for proper burial until May 6, 2002.

[3]   US laws enacted during this time to ostensibly curb violent protests from radical immigrants involved in Communist activities.

[4]   This result is from a sample of 893 Black women. It is not clear that the study only tested for antibodies to the virus (noting exposure, not necessarily infection), which rendered a public misinterpretation of the data (Crute, 2010).

[5]   The article was removed within the same week.

[6]   In this viral video (also created in October 2010) a puppet with an afro sings a love song to her hair. Joey Mazzarino, head writer of Sesame Street, penned the segment as a celebration/encouragement for his 5-year Black daughter who began to admire the long, blonde hair of her dolls. As of February 1, 2012, the video has had over 3.3 million views.

[7]   Black Girls Rock! Inc. celebrated their 4th year in October 2010, with an awards celebration hosted by Black Entertainment Television.

METHODS

If you have come to help me, you are wasting your time. But if you have come because your liberation is bound up with mine, then let us work together.
– Lilla Watson (Aboriginal activist group, Queensland, circa 1970)

In this project, I am aware that I am not a (birth) mother. This distinction seemed important to make so the women I worked with understood I had not positioned myself as a 'parent expert.' In our first Saturday morning, meeting I greeted them as a child of the South Side of Chicago, a daughter of CPS teachers, a community activist, and a graduate student. I gave them the space to approach me as they saw fit. Some related to me as a researcher – Sonia asking me point blank – "I want to know what *you* are reading" some related to me as another warm body in action; and others related to me as a sister and a daughter. I would not come in and sympathetically nod because these women did not need judgmental affirmation nor did they need to be fixed. However, I did relate as a woman who wants to support *our* children. This afforded me an intimate space of collecting data even when there were no pencils or recorders present.

I believe many of the mothers I met at SSCES saw me as a marker of success. Not only am I a product of CPS and a child of a 'whatever it takes' mother, I am a Sankofa[1] bird: a woman who remembers and returns. I am a Black woman from Chicago, claiming my identity as a feminist researcher – an activist – while learning how to be the Mother(s) I have participated with my entire life (Villenas, 1996). Toward the end of our first meeting, I candidly admitted to them, "I know who you are, but I don't see you women in my research." Light bulbs burst in my brain as I continued, "I think I want to do my dissertation here." The room exploded in celebration. I told them I would pray about it and confer with my advisor, but there was something in those initial moments too powerful for words. And they knew it. One of the mothers – Maya – assured me without question: "Oh, you'll be back." Considering the charge of Madison (2005), I reflexively asked, *so who am I to tell their stories?* I am a researcher, an othermother, a sister, and a daughter – writing my story of *their* stories. We are all coparticipants in this project.

"I KNOW WHO YOU ARE BUT...": EPISTEMOLOGY

When I met these women, I immediately saw the gap between the mothers I knew growing up and the mothers I read through dominant discourses. While I had been taught by my family to critically examine who I am as a Black person, and later as a Black woman, I had yet to examine the complexities of class. There were certain things I took for granted – that regardless of where anyone lived or worked, I believed there were just certain things Black people did within every family that had nothing to do with money. Some of these universal truths and actions were: being sure to come in the house before the street lights came on; standing in long lines at the Catholic charity for blocks of cheese and milk; referring to everyone as Ms., Mr., or Aunt and Uncle – even if they weren't blood-related; a weekend filled with Soul Train on Saturdays; church on Sundays; and mothers who either showed up at school or got in your face at home. Across all of the homes I was raised, these were constants. Therefore, the "crack mother" and the "Welfare Queen" were foreign to me. I first regarded their media images (see *Losing Isaiah, Boyz in the Hood*) as two-dimensional caricatures or anomalies that existed in a benign subculture.

However, as I began to read education literature regarding the achievement gap, most of it pointed to families of color and the lack of parent involvement. In fact, a child who is considered "at-risk for school failure" (U.S. Department of Education, 2006) is defined in terms of demographic or historical characteristics associated with an increased likelihood of adverse outcomes. A March 2006 report by the National Center for Educational Statistics outlines three at-risk categories: status, academic, and behavior. These categories include being a "minority" coming from a low-income home (noting that nearly 76% of Black children living in large metropolitan areas, live in neighborhoods that have higher poverty rates than those found in the urban neighborhoods of the poorest White children; Law and Policy Group, Inc., 2008); come from a home where English is not the primary language; and/or fail to develop a sense that schooling is important to future life success. These findings clearly echo the Moynihan Report and subsequent work.

'Closing' the achievement gap – noted by Critical Race Theory scholars as the "educational debt" (Ladson-Billings, 2006) – has become a priority of the American Education agenda as noted by the US Secretary of Education: "The achievement gap is unacceptable. Education is the civil rights issue of our generation. It is the only way to make good on the American promise of equality" (Duncan, 2010). This statement is driven alongside over 31,400 journal articles highlighted by Google Scholar with "at-risk" as the buzzphrase for reform. Books and edited collections such as *Words at Work and Play* (Brice Heath, 1983); *Young, Gifted, and Black: Promoting High Achievement Among African-American Students* (Perry, Steele, & Hilliard, 2004); *Funds of Knowledge: Theorizing Practices in Households, Communities, and Classroom* (Gonzalez, Moll, & Amanti, 2005); and *Racism, Research, and Educational Reform: Voices from the City* (Dowdy & Wynne, 2005), have contributed to the body of work that draws relationships between parent involvement, cultural competency, and academic achievement. Therefore, it is essential to understand the circuitry of these efforts with respect to Black families/mothers.

The need for parent involvement has been acknowledged as federal funding has been allocated for family-engaging activities. The Department of Education has proposed to increase these funds and the reauthorization of the Elementary and

Secondary Education Act (1965, 2011) has opened to review of the existing parent involvement provisions (Chang & Williams, 2011). However, "traditional research on parental involvement neglects the ways in which parental engagement is a social practice, sustained through active participation and dialogue in a social world" (Barton, Drake, Perez, St. Louis, & George, 2004, p. 6). Therefore, the push for parent involvement is more indicative of what the *school* needs to perform well as opposed to advancing the needs of the families. In this way, I saw my role in developing the Parent University as an opportunity to develop holistic measures and activities that would incorporate the parents, students, community, teachers, and school staff as equally participating stakeholders.

Black feminist thought. In addition to my research of the parent involvement literature, I revisited Black Feminist Thought as a tool of inquiry. Employing a feminist methodology was/is critical because of its commitment to social justice. A feminist method in social research works to dismantle power structures and recognizes that women experience oppression and exploitation based on race, class, and sexual orientation much differently than others (Reinharz, 1992). Taking steps further, "involving much more than simply the counseling of existing social science source, the placing of ideas and experiences of women of color in the center of analysis requires invoking a different epistemology" (Hill-Collins, 2004a, p. 49). My experiences in this research have brought me to the realization that doing fieldwork is always personal, so I take particular care in examination of positionality. "We must distinguish between what has been said about subordinated groups in the dominant discourse, and what such groups might say about themselves if given the opportunity" (Hill-Collins, 2004a, p. 49). Therefore – as noted in Chapter 1 – I had to ask, how often do individuals interact with Black mothers and in what context? I had to remember my own stories and open myself to those I had not heard/listened to. Black Feminist Thought provided a lens for me to learn from these women.

Dominant discourse would have us to believe that there is only a specific type of woman that is allowed to speak (e.g., Mammy; sassy, strict disciplinarian; or professional-career woman). The market is full of books by both women and men who are proud of their 'Mama' however, the same market is a bit thin on work of Black mothers offering any advice or wisdom in raising children/families. Black mothers are promoted in 'out of the ordinary' success stories such as *Mama Rock's Rules: Ten Lessons for Raising a Household of Successful Children* (Rock & Graham, 2009) by Rose Rock, who not only raised Chris Rock (*SNL* Alum, first solo Black male host of the *Academy Awards*, and the most frequent male celebrity on *The Oprah Winfrey Show*), one of her ten biological children as well as 17 foster children. We can also count former CBS News anchor and breast cancer survivor/spokesperson, Rene Syler, who penned *Good Enough Mother* two years prior. There is nothing inherently "magical"[2] about what these women tell us – Rock simply shares what she learned from her mother regarding love, autonomy, honesty, and discipline; Syler shares what she has learned from her mistakes. However, these works do mark the expansion of a vital canon and acknowledge the importance of Black mothers having a stage to speak and to be affirmed. Again, none of these stories are new; however, the SSCES parent sessions made clear to me the necessity for visibility in traditionally marginalized spaces. During her 2014 keynote address, bell hooks reflects upon her very first work and the decisions she made throughout her academic career:

> Indeed, what these [other] folks heard as anger, I heard as clear, bold language speaking truth to power… I chose years ago to cultivate a style of writing that was clear – one that make use of plain language, relying on everyday speech. I wanted to make the writing be as simple as possible, to serve – via my writing choices – those who have the least access to academic discourse. [This] was for me, a gesture of political solidarity.

It is then imperative during this time that we not only elevate the perspectives of those who have been rewarded by mainstream media but even (if not especially) those mothers who cross our paths every day. If their stories are not told now, while Black mothers are criminalized and vilified, we will build our archives upon the myths of scientific research and the lives of people who will always seemingly be out of our reach.

Counternarratives: Critical race theory.   These voices of Black women, written as narratives, or rather as narratives counter to the dominant discourse discussed in Chapter 2, peel back the masks that seek to "conceal their humanity," (Delgado & Stefancic, 2001 p. 42). This work borrows the tool of counternarratives, a widely understood component of Critical Race Theory (CRT) which "aims to cast doubt on the validity of accepted premises or myths, especially ones held by the majority" (p. 144). This fits well with BFT as both a theory and a method because "unlike some academic disciplines CRT contains an activist dimension" (p. 3).

CRT is an outgrowth of critical legal studies, radical feminism, and conventional civil rights thought. It dates back to the mid-70's and builds on the work of scholars such as the late Derrick Bell, Alan Freeman, Richard Delgado, and Kimberlé Crenshaw. Critical race theory operates from several tenets, which vary slightly across generation – realist and idealist (Delgado & Stefancic, 2001; Carlton Parsons, Rhodes, & Brown, 2011) and application (i.e., outgrowths such as LatCrit, TribCrit, Asian Crit, etc.). However, the following are generally agreed upon tenets that scholars work from: (1) permanence of racism (2) social construction of race (3) critique of liberalism (4) interest convergence (5) whiteness as property, (6) intersectionality and (7) counternarratives/storytelling. Other areas that have received incredible attention regard microaggressions and retrenchment (Crenshaw, Gotanda, Peller, & Thomas, 1995; Wing, 2003; Taylor, Gillborn, & Ladson-Billings, 2009; Lynn & Dixson, 2013). It is important to note that the work of Gloria Ladson-Billings and William F. Tate (1995), introduced CRT to Education.

Crenshaw is credited with coining the term "intersectionality" upon the publication of two groundbreaking articles that sought to provide a theoretical space regarding the law's inability to make women's experience of discrimination through race, class, and gender visible (1989). In this vein, I use counternarratives as a dual lens to examine who benefits from the proliferation of dominant stories and how Black mothers may create and claim their own.

> History books, Sunday sermons, and even case law contribute to a cultural hegemony that makes it difficult for reformers to make race an issue. How to bridge the gap in thinking between persons of goodwill whose experiences, perspectives, and backgrounds are radically different is a great challenge... critical writers use counternarratives to challenge, displace, or mock these pernicious narratives and beliefs... they reveal that others have similar experiences [and] can name a type of discrimination; once named, it can be combated. (Delgado & Stefancic, 2001, pp. 39–40, 43)

This is the function of counternarratives in *We Can Speak for Ourselves.*

Black feminist, writer, and mother Audre Lorde writes, "as we learn to bear the intimacy of scrutiny and to flourish within it, as we learn to use the products of that scrutiny for power within our living, those fears which rule our lives and form our silences begin to lose their control over us" (p. 36, 1977/2007). In a larger sense, we seek to understand that the issues of race and subordination of Black mothers is not simply the problem of Black mothers, but is endemic in how we function and prepare our children to function within the whole of society.

QUALITATIVE METHODS

A qualitative research methodology was required for this project to construct a counternarrative of Black mothers. Qualitative research typically centers on relatively small samples selected purposefully to permit inquiry into and understanding of a phenomenon in depth (Patton, 2001). This method seeks to understand the social phenomena from the perspectives of those involved, to contextualize issues in theory (particularly sociocultural theory) and sometimes to transform or change social conditions (Glesne, 2006, p. 4). I have selected an ethnographic approach to gain a greater understanding of the experiences of Black mothers in an urban community of Chicago. Use of a critical ethnographic lens requires an examination of institutional and social structures.

I take my lead from qualitative inquiry, with respect to critical and post-critical ethnography because of my politics on issues of positionality, subjectivity, voice, and advocacy. D. Soyini Madison (2011) defines critical ethnography as social justice and risk coupled with truth and translation. Much like the reciprocal relationship between parents and teachers, she asks that the same take place between the researchers and participants with a major focus on the reflexivity of the researcher. In *Critical Ethnography* (2005), Madison poses five questions for reflexive consideration:

1. How is the specificity of the local story relevant to the broader meanings and operations of the human condition?

33

2. How do we create and maintain a dialogue of collaboration in our research projects between ourselves and Others?
3. How do we predict consequences or evaluate our own potential to do harm?
4. How do we reflect upon and evaluate our own purpose, intentions, and frames of analysis as researchers?
5. How – in what location or through what intervention – will your work make the greatest contribution to equity, freedom, and justice?

By these principles and the very act of writing, researching and living exposes the fact that ethnography teaches the researcher as much about herself as it does about her participants and their environment (Goodall, 2000). I provide special consideration to the latter two questions in Chapter 6.

As a Black woman conducting research with Black women, I employ critical ethnography as a tool against observer bias, also referred to as mesearch. Certainly there are shared cultural experiences – Black women are not a monolith – and there are other layers of our identities that must be recognized and sometimes negotiated to create meaningful relationships. These women "are inspirational, breathing new life into the work of teaching, research, and living. They are memories that transform; a place within and without that feeds our ability to engage new metaphors and practices in our work" (Dillard, 2008, pp. 90–91). For this reason, I do not minimize who I am in this work because that would betray the entire body. Paula Groves (2003) writes,

the dissatisfaction with the requirement to repress the researcher's visceral emotions, identities, and positionality has led to the growth of critical ethnography, as researchers recognize the irony of corporeal repression in a paradigm of embodied research… the study of and advocacy for the oppressed should come from the oppressed themselves. Not only could studying one's own inspire powerful research designs, but in a critical paradigm it is desired, as it can potentially escape some of the traps of 'exoticizing the other' that is frequently found in conventional ethnography. (p. 104)

Therefore, these mother's willingness to participate in this work is received as an honor to the work it builds upon, the lives they live, and the children we love.

ETHICAL RESEARCH

The process of contacting and collecting information from the mothers was approved by the Institutional Review Board (IRB) guided by the Office of Human Research Ethics (OHRE). This process included a submission of an application that details the step-by-step data collection process and protection/confidentiality of the participants; the recruitment letter to members of The Beacons; the adult consent form; and interview protocols. These are ethical measures instituted in 1979, resulting from The Belmont Report.[3] This 11-member commission – which included two Black women, Patricia A., King, J. D. and the late Dorothy Irene Height – was to "identify the basic ethical principles that should underlie the conduct of biomedical and behavioral research involving human subjects and to develop guidelines which should be followed to assure that such research is conducted in accordance with those principles" (U.S. Department of Health and Human Services).

The Belmont Report identifies three basic ethical principles: Respect for Persons, Beneficence, Justice. This commission assembled in response to the Tuskegee Syphilis Study (1932–1972), also known as the Tuskegee Experiment. This study, conducted by the U.S. Public Health Service, used approximately 600 Black men (400 infected and 200 control) from a rural area of Alabama as test subjects to observe the natural progression of untreated syphilis over the course of 40 years. The participants were not clearly informed of their status and were refused and prevented from receiving safe treatments – while penicillin was validated as an effective cure for the disease 15 years after the study began (Heller, 1972). The effect of this experiment infected more than the men, but their wives and unborn children as well and was malevolently linked to sexual behaviors within Black families and communities. John Heller, *Director of the Public Health Service's Division of Venereal Diseases* defends the study asserting, "they were subjects, not patients; clinical material, not sick people" (Jones, 1993, p. 179). The fatal impact of this experiment has been widely disputed; however, the immorality of the design and execution is clear.

While The Tuskegee Experiment raised the consciousness of the science and medical communities, during this same time frame – in 1951 – Henrietta Lacks was diagnosed with cancer. Healthy and cancerous samples were removed from her cervix without permission and long after her death (that same year when she was buried in an unmarked grave,) these cells have generated breakthrough discoveries for biomedical research with respect to cancer, AIDS, and gene mapping as a start (Skloot, 2011; Lacks & Lacks, 2013). The violation of this Black woman's body and the subsequent violation of her children falls in line with the scientific quests performed 150 years prior demonstrated with Sara Baartman. This context is necessary to underscore the wrestling of conducting empirical research as a Black woman (Jeffries, 2003) and the necessity of an institutional system that requires constant transparency and accountability.

INTERVIEWS

The participants of this project are the mothers I worked with in the parent organization of SSCES, The Beacons, during the 2010 Summer. While the initial roster lists over 50 women, I worked closely with the executive board and committee members of the group, which was a network of approximately 15. This provided a substantial range for purposeful sampling and for this project, five of the latter agreed to participate in this project. These women range in age, class, geography, occupation, number/genders/ages of children, schooling experiences, and marital statuses (see Appendix I). Two sets of interviews were conducted between October 2011 and February 2012. This time range was necessary to accommodate travel and holiday schedules. For the first round, I returned to Chicago and conducted 1–1.5-hour interviews with three of these mothers while a fourth interview was conducted over the phone.[4] These are women who had already expressed a commitment to this project and produced a fair range of experiences, particularly regarding their relationships with the school. Their knowledge, experience, and expertise allowed me to "learn a great deal about issues of central importance to the purpose of my research" (Glesne, 2006, p. 34) and I developed an interview guide[5] that gave space for more nuances in their roles as women, mothers, and advocates for their children. Each mother selected a time of day and location that was most comfortable and accommodating for them. For the second round of interviews, two of the previous mothers from the initial project participated in addition to one more. These interviews ranged in length from 1 to 2 hours and were guided by open-ended questions that were structured according to the five types of motherwork (Hill-Collins, 2004a) described in Chapter 1:

1. Women Centered Networks
2. Mothers and Daughters
3. Community Othermothers and Political Activism
4. Motherhood as a Symbol of Power
5. The View from the Inside

CODING

Coding was an essential part of my data analysis that allowed me to identify salient themes and patterns. According to Coffey and Atkinson (1996), "in practice, coding can be thought of as a range of approaches that aid the organization, retrieval, and interpretation of data" (p. 27). The three approaches to coding that I employed were in vivo coding, sociologically constructed coding, and open coding. The initial approach I employed during data analysis was open coding. Open coding is identified as an 'open' process because it "allow[ed] me to engage in exploration of my data without making any prior assumptions about what I might discover" (Kerlin, 2000). After employing open coding, I moved to more selective approaches: in vivo coding and sociologically constructed coding. In vivo coding "refers to the codes that derive from the terms and the language used by social actors in the field, or in the course of the interviews (Coffey & Atkinson, 1996, p. 32)." In vivo coding allowed me to inductively engage with the participant's narrative. On the other hand, sociologically constructed coding allowed me "to identify themes, patterns, events, and actions that are of my interest and that provide a means of organizing data sets (p. 32)." Because I am invested in this research, my positionality is evident in my data analysis as I have identified themes and patterns that reflect my own lived experiences (Moore, 2009).

I conducted three sets of interpretations from the data. First, I arranged the transcripts according to schooling narratives in a thematic and chronological order: their own, their children, their expectations for the future. From here, several codes were generated such as "living in Chicago," "what my mother did," "not enough time," "being vocal," "embarrassment." After these patterns were revealed, the data was analyzed again, creating new patterns, and I was able to develop common subheadings. From this emerged four themes: "Defining Mother," "Preparing Children," "Navigating Institutions," and "Other." There are two dominant narratives; three that complement, complicate, and enhance the other narratives (all of which are shared in Chapter 4); and the narrative of an imagined "Other" that is examined in Chapter 5. They are all ordered by the dates interviewed with the two dominant narratives presented first.

NARRATIVES

The interviews were analyzed as narratives. I used narrative to introduce and represent the stories these women shared with me regarding their experiences as mother, daughter, teacher, student, and advocate. Narrative inquiry is one way we make meaning of our experiences. More than method or theory, narrative inquiry is about understanding stories. I contend that narratives provide understanding of experience (MacIntyre, 1984), welcome contradictions that emerge in the narration and representation of stories (Clandinin & Connelly, 2000) and allow readers to honor the particular (Noblit, 1999).

According to Coffey and Atkinson (1996), "narratives have rather specific, distinct structures with formal and identifiable properties (p. 57)." Therefore, I used a formal narrative analysis to structure and interpret my data. Coffey and Atkinson (1996) refer to William Labov's (1982) sociolinguistic approach as a method to interpret a story. In my research, I used Labov's sociolinguistic approach, specifically the evaluation model, to

> identify how the participant tells their story the way they do: how the participant gives the events that recount shape; how the participant makes a point; how the participant 'packages' the narrated events and their reaction to them, and how the participant articulates their narrative with the audience or audiences that hear them. (p. 58)

There are certainly rhythms apparent in the way each woman speaks. I attempted to capture this through punctuation and formatting. At any point of tension or light-heartedness, there is a lot of laughter, pauses for self-reflection or assessment and quite a few "mmmhms" from me. These are noted most in places where they shifted their tone or train of thought. I kept the narratives in the first person to maintain the sense that they are speaking for themselves to a direct audience. Connelly and Clandinin (1990) note narrative inquiry is a "process of collaboration involving mutual storytelling and restorying as the research proceeds... the researcher needs to be aware of constructing a relationship in which both voices are heard" (p. 4). In restorying, fluidly and fullness of the narrative takes precedence above chronological exactness of the data collected.

Moreover, this form of analysis provides a respite from the "death dance of dependence" (Grande, 2004, p. 2) upon the master's tools (Lorde, 1977/2007). Hill-Collins (2004a) writes,

> personal narratives, autobiographical statements, poetry, fiction, and other personalized statements have all been used by women of color to express self-defined standpoints on mothering and motherhood. Such knowledge reflects the authentic standpoint of subordinated groups. Therefore, placing these sources in the center and supplementing them with statistics, historical material, and other knowledge produced to justify the interests of ruling elites should create new themes and angles of vision. (p. 49)

POETRY

This project is about how each woman stories herself. In this spirit, I have received each of these women as poets, and I retell *our* stories as gifts of "...true knowledge and therefore, lasting action..." (Lorde, p. 37, 1977/2007). Again, Audre Lorde tells us, "for women... poetry is not a luxury. It is a vital necessity of our existence. It forms the quality of the light within which we predicate our hopes and dreams toward survival and change..." (p. 37, 1977/2007). Just as action is the gift of Black Feminist Thought, poetry is the gift of language. Therefore, as a woman and an artist, the inclusion of poetry in this project is just as important as the theoretical framework and analysis.

> The emergence of poetry within the research process is connected not only to the overall increase in arts-based practices but also to broader epistemological and theoretical insights such as those posed by postmodern and poststructural theory. Feminist and other politically motivated research may be interested in the political possibilities of poetry as well as its ability to "stay true" to the speech patterns of interview respondents. (Leavy, 2009, pp. 64–65)

In Chapter 6, I offer a brief poetic transcription of the mothers' narratives. Qualitative researcher Corrine Glesne writes, "poetic transcription blurs the accepted boundaries between art and science [by] exploring the shapes of inter-subjectivity, and examining issues of power and authority, including that of researcher/author" (p. 204). This form of writing is not used throughout this work; however, I provide a rationale here for its use to set a precedent for interpretations in future projects.

The pseudonyms of the mothers presented here are all names of contemporary Black female poets whose performances range from presidential inaugurations to the Apollo stage in Harlem, New York: Maya Angelou, Sonia Sanchez, Carolyn M. Rodgers, Nikki Giovanni, Jill Scott, and Deja K. Taylor. While the children were not interviewed for this project, they were certainly part of the conversations. Their daughters are named for African ethnic groups, and their sons are named for African emperors (see Appendix IV).

VALIDITY

In *Becoming Qualitative Researchers,* Glesne (2006) states that validity is an issue we should consider "during research design as well in the midst of data collection" (p. 35). She lists several verification procedures one can employ to address the issue of research validity. The procedure I used is member checking. Glesne (2006) describes member checking as "sharing interview transcripts, analytical thoughts, and/or drafts of the final report with research participants to make sure you are representing them and their ideas accurately" (p. 36). Member checking has helped me verify the trustworthiness of my data collection and analysis.

After the first round of interviews with the mothers, three of them corresponded with me through email and phone to share moments they forgot to discuss. This was an opportunity to recall what we had already discussed so they could offer room for clarification as well as carry the conversations further. In other cases, I offered to share my interview notes with the mothers, to which Maya said, "no honey! I've seen your notes. I'm sure you captured me as thoroughly as possible. I don't need to read all of that." Lastly, I am in constant communication with the majority of these women because they want to continue to share accomplishments of their children. This is in addition to exercising open access channels of social media and the need to vent as Black women about the heightened awareness of our images and lifestyles in everyday exchanges. The latter has afforded me the opportunity to communicate with them regarding current issues, allowing us to revisit and check our previous discussions.

RECIPROCITY

A moment that has never left me is from an American Educational Studies Association (AESA) conference I attended as a new graduate student. Bettina Love (2012) presented research from her dissertation, which is an ethnographic project of high school students' ideas on gender, race, sexuality, and education, which are formed by Hip Hop. With respect to her role as an ethnographer, her most powerful statement was, "these girls gave me a Ph.D.; I had to ask myself, what am I giving them?"

I risked my standing with the administration of the school – learning how and when to share information that affected them as parents while they risked not only their vulnerability but that of their children as well. They first trusted me as secretary for the meetings and then trusted me to take notes on their lives. Our conversations were filled with 'mama stories,' references to academic journal articles, current news, relationships with men, and updates on the children we take care of. On more than one occasion one of the mothers would say to me, "it's crazy that no one's ever asked me these things before… I've never had a conversation like this before." I would then convey my appreciation by thanking them for better preparing me to be a mother.

I entered these women's space performing different roles (researcher, employee, daughter, othermother) and asked that they provide me with the performance of mother. As spaces grew and transformed around us, we became coparticipants, and I was asked to give as much as I received. In fact, about five minutes into my interview with Nikki, she paused the conversation and said, "I'm gonna take notes."

Because the mothers and I were actively creating community, I looked to *The Quilt* (Alexander Craft et al., 2007) as a reflexive guide while reviewing my analysis of the transcripts. In this article, sister/artist/activist/othermother/scholars Renée Alexander Craft, Meida McNeal, Mshaï S. Mwangola provide a collective list they call: "Tenets of a Twenty-First Century Feminist Ethnography" (pp. 79–80). It is reminiscent of what Alice Walker (1983) defines as being "involved in work her soul must have" (p. 241). This requires that I examine my positionality as an inside/outsider and a raced/gendered body/agent capable of healing, harming, and transcendence. It also required that I continue to tend to these spaces after this project concluded.

REFLEXIVE JOURNAL

Journaling throughout this process was crucial to capture both the shifts in my perspectives – as well as the mothers' – and our evolving relationships. During the initial step of this project – where I was contracted to develop the Parent University – I was additionally selected as a blogger for my fellowship organization. Through an assignment of about two blog entries per week, they were interested in knowing more about the personal and professional experiences of the Fellows who held various positions throughout the country. As one of the few Black people in the fellowship, who worked directly in a school with parents and community partners, I was very conscious of how I would publically blog about my work, the relationships that developed and more importantly my shifting lens throughout the 10-week process. I used the blog – this first reflexive journal – to write about how

Blog entry for July 14, 2010. When [my fellowship director] Leigh, phoned to ask if I would be interested in developing a Parent University, I was excited for a new adventure. I have worked in the Chicago public and charter school system since 1998. Generally speaking, I have had the luxury of simply worrying about lesson plans of a group of 10 or 20 students at a time; however, in my last position as afterschool director, I had to hire staff, coordinate professional development meetings, recruit community partners, serve as disciplinarian, facilitate student leadership meetings, manage *all* the evening curricula and of course, have parent meetings. I was a tour-de-force running around that school in slacks and heels (which I often traded for sneakers.)

I can honestly say that I loved my parents. Even the toughest cookies would bend and melt with the enthusiasm and success of their child or at least with the understanding that I would do everything in my power to make sure their child was in a safe environment to foster his/her maximum potential. In a school that was still adjusting to its' gentrified surroundings, new teachers, and standard testing expectations, my parents became my strongest allies. I was never alone. Even when I did not see them, I knew they were just around a corner and had the same high expectations for me as *we* collectively had for their children. It was memories of these parents that came to mind when Leigh said, "Parent University." She knew I loved community work and wanted to be involved with a qualitative research project. She is a great match-maker.

I connected with the Regional Director of the charter organization within a few days, and we conversed as if we'd known one another for years. It was such a natural conversation. We were knee-deep into programming ideas when she asked me if I foresaw any challenges. My enthusiasm was immediately pierced by a memory I often try to dismiss.

There had been one parent that did not bend or melt. In fact, she was fortified with fire and rage by the time I reached her in the main office. She seemed to want my head *and* a pound of flesh. In a boisterous voice, she questioned my integrity and credentials as well as those of my staff all while making bombastic, idle threats. The truth of it all was buried under her years of hurt and frustration, which had *nothing* to do with me, and she needed a punching bag. I stood there, as a steel light post in a storm, praying not to be ripped from my position, praying the staff members did not notice me blinking at tears. Days later, when the dust settled, and there was no apology, I nursed an open wound while trying to imagine alternate courses for that event. However, it was over. I had to realize, that was just one battle. That was just one parent. I still had 200 other children and families to service. I had to remember that I really did love my parents. And they were my biggest allies...

Parents play one of *the most* important roles in how we choose to educate (and reform,) yet they seem to be absent in a vast majority of the research I've read – except when we are looking at what they *don't* do. I am made more aware of the "pound of flesh" parents because they seem to be the "squeaky wheels" but *these* parents are working so diligently and seamlessly behind the scenes that you can easily forget that they are the backbone of the whole operation.

my presence transformed the space of the school and challenged my assumptions as both an insider and outsider.

When the fellowship concluded, I continued this journal privately. I was able to write more about the women themselves – how I saw them, beautiful and flawed. I wrote about how many times I felt like I was in the way. I wrote about how angry I was about some of the administration's decisions. I wrote about times I felt like "The Spook Who Sat By the Door."[6] I wrote about the discomfort of these women trusting me with personal experiences that I knew I would choose, shape, and present to a public audience. I wrote about how much Maya reminded me of so many women I'd grown up with and how Nikki reminded me of a big sister I totally would have looked up to. I wrote about being an othermother – an organic role I assumed having worked in various school and community institutions for over ten years – where my children referred to me as *Shangazi*.[7] I also wrote about my own mother – a lot.

GIVING VOICE

In 2011, I attended a session of AESA entitled: "Culturally Responsive Research Approaches: Distinctive Means of Infusing Silenced Voices." After the panelists, Donna Deyhle, Thandeka Chapman, and David Stovall spoke, a burning question regarding my participants made me thrust my hand into the air. I shared that I was working on a project with women whose lives are familiar to me as my own and my concern was carrying the responsibility of transmitting their voices ethically and authentically because I am taking them into a new space. "I can't say that I am *giving* these women voices – they can speak for themselves." Dr. Stovall interrupted me with, "that's it right there. *These women can speak for themselves*. You are just sharing the conversation."

LIMITATIONS

I was brought to SSCES on a paid contract for a specific assignment. This was my initial engagement. I performed as a daughter and othermother to leverage the power dynamics and to be in a position where I could *learn*. However, despite my best face, in many ways I was tied to the administration as well as to an outside institution. Then, for the purposes of this project, I returned with yet another institutional affiliation, the University, and asked these women to fit into my boxes (e.g., deadlines, IRB, theoretical frameworks). I was aware that when the recorder powered on, and pencil was in my hand, we were shifting our relationships and boundaries. I tried to be as transparent as possible with each mother about my position and purpose. However, they ultimately made a decision about which performance they choose for my academic audience. We danced according to the previous/growing intimacies we shared with one another; I pushed and pulled in a space of familiarity. Again, I was in a position to *learn*. Just as everyone else, I entered a conversation that started long before I arrived. These mothers had a discourse, literature, frameworks, familial theories, and fruitful networks; it was imperative that I took my lead from them.

MAYA, NIKKI, CAROLYN, JILL, SONIA

The following chapter presents the raw data of each mothers' narrative. I begin with a brief introduction our relationship and how it developed through this project. What follows are the puzzle pieces of the transcripts, which includes bits of the body language, silences, and even my responses – as we understand just as much can be gleaned from what is spoken as from what is *not* spoken. Spending time with these women meant absorbing the pictures of grandparents framed on the walls, the bouncing volume of television in the background as a son played with his friend, an intimate ritual of a family dinner. When Carolyn asked, "is it okay if Khoi comes too," of course I agreed. Her question acknowledged that this was a project focused on her life but also that she felt comfortable enough to share the space with her youngest daughter. During my time with Nikki, another parent came by to drop her son off as she went to work the overnight shift. Nikki introduced me with so much excitement: 'She's interviewing me about being a mother. You should call her so she can interview you too!' Because none of the mothers responded to my presence as an interruption, I simply had to move in step with their lives. The narrative crafting of their voices works to mirror the fluid and staccato rhythms of an ordinary day.

NOTES

[1] This Adinkra symbol – most prevalent in West Africa – illustrates a bird looking backward with the egg of the future in her beak. She is remembering and preserving the past as she continuously and protectively moves forward.

[2] The Magical Negro is an archetypal mass media image of a Black person dramatically employed to teach, support, and serendipitously transform American White society.

[3] The full title is: The Belmont Report: Ethical Principles and Guidelines for the Protection of Human Subjects of Research, Report of the National Commission for the Protection of Human Subjects of Biomedical and Behavioral Research – April 18, 1979.

[4] See Appendix II for initial interview guide.

[5] See Appendix III for second interview guide.

[6] *The Spook Who Sat By the Door* (1969/1989) is a work of fiction by Sam Greenlee that describes a Black male who utilizes his skills and training as a government agent to develop young men on the South Side of Chicago as "Freedom Fighters."

[7] This is the Swahili term for "aunt."

CHAPTER 4

THE MOTHERS

MAYA

In our first meeting, Maya introduced herself as the "cheer mom." Her daughter's many activities and accomplishments took precedent in every conversation. Everything she said was matter-of-fact and she spoke with a smile either on her face or in her voice. She did not directly talk about her job but made it clear that her schedule was tight and not to be played with. She kept her calendar in hand, noting when and where she was available to meet or volunteered to take on leadership positions. She often vocalized her commitment not only to her child but also to the success of the school.

Maya reminded me most of my own mother. She was older when she gave birth to her only child – Mursi – and has raised her with wisdom she admits she did not have in her 20s or 30s. She believes raising her child is truly a gift and responsibility of God that she does not take lightly. She states in no uncertain terms that her child is her priority and that she will make whatever sacrifices necessary to ensure her success. In addition to her faith, she has made the choice to raise her daughter in the same community that she grew up in – with the very same community mother that raised her. Although this is an area that has been known for high gang and drug activity, she places great value on the fact that her daughter is able to live in the same building with her sisters, nieces, and nephews.

I interacted with Maya several times throughout my work at the school. She was always very encouraging and whenever I was present, she relinquished her role as secretary. When I apologized for "being a researcher," she told me to be proud of what I did and that I made her job easier. I felt like I knew quite a bit about her before our first interview, but in the comforts of her home, the first thing she opened up to me about was her relationship with God and the importance of His guidance in raising her daughter. This set the tone for our time together and made me feel more like I was with my own family. Both interviews for this project lasted over 3.5 hours and took place in her home, after work. Mursi was always present – either asking for permission to do something or to catch me up on what was happening in her life.

Learning mother. My mom was married to my dad yet she was a single mom and she raised three kids essentially by herself with the community. Like, my grandfather's sister would help my mom because being in public school was not ideal at that time for us. Especially in this neighborhood because I grew up on 51st and Wabash (*she points toward the window, out to the neighborhood*) and the Blackstone Rangers and

45

all of that were prominent back when I was in school. We were in public school initially – on State Street and I saw a guy get killed and went home and told my mom that. She just could not take it anymore and my great-aunt that considered my mom her favorite niece, made the decision.

[My aunt] was extremely active in St. Mary Magdalene Patronage. She was Catholic and we were Baptist, but she offered my mom assistance with tuition and back then tuition was extremely affordable. Back then patronage was extremely huge and very, very profitable for our community because it was a community taking care of community – that is what patronage was. If your kid or your family needed something and I had a business – if you could help me, I helped you. And so back then in the 60s and the 70s that is what kept the Black Catholic schools going and the community flourishing because it was about the communities. The neighborhood restaurant and grocery store employed the teenage boys. They did stock, they did gas stations and wasn't nobody on the street and when you *were* on the street it was playtime and you could ride your bikes. I mean I never rode my bike just in the neighborhood. Living on 51st and Wabash we could go to McCormick Place or we would ride to Evanston[1] during the day! We did not have to stay in the neighborhood as long as you were in before the street lights came on. Now, so, my aunt helped my mom put us in Catholic school. And that changed our lives because my mom was emphatic that we were not going to be neighborhood kids – there was really not a whole lot wrong with it, but what was going on back in the 60s and 70s, you know. [I] grew up on the wrong side of the tracks but my mother gave us the education on the other side. You know, and because of that – that is why I push. I tried Catholic school for Mursi. And actually St. Mary's wanted me to put her in there, but I was like yall are too expensive. They were like, well if you come do community (*her voice trails*) ugh…. I am not Catholic! I suffered through grammar school and high school doing everything that I had to do – because you had community service with Catholic school – I mean with the Girl Scouts – I was a Girl Scout for 10 years at St. Mary's. Charm school, cheerleading, all of that came through the parish.

And when we cheered they did not know how to judge Black cheerleaders. Yeah! (*She responds to my raised eyebrows.*) And said it. And we beat [other teams] hands down, but we were not recognized because they did not know how to judge us because we weren't doing this (*she stiffens her arms and claps very methodically*) and we weren't doing that. You know. And we were (*her arms begin to move comfortably*), we had rhythm and style. There was flow to our cheers. There wasn't anything ghetto, but it was flow. We were doing what we naturally knew how to do. We cheered like they cheered, but we had rhythm when we did and the first time we heard [we couldn't win], we went back to St. Mary's and we all sat in the gym because we were emphatic: we were not cheering again. We were not going to deal with that. And it was the mamas and the daddies that said, "oh yeah, you are going to cheer" or "oh we are going back, and you are going to keep going back until they learn how to judge you!"

So that broke our barriers. I was not raised Black or White – I was raised that this is a multicultural world. You better learn how to deal with it from grammar school because our parents pushed us out there, our parents exposed us. Girl Scouts – there weren't no Black girls in Girl Scouts! I won Miss Girl Scout 1976 and we went to Washington and Philadelphia and at that time in 1976, Helen Jean Ford was the first Black Ms. America.[2] Her mom worked with my mom at Provident Hospital. The old Provident Hospital that all of us worked at. All of my family and I had a chance to meet her. She came to the ceremony where I was crowned and I told everybody that I was her little sister and then they did a big thing for the city and the state with Girl Scouts of America at the amphitheater where they recognized me and she let me wear her crown and her sash. Yep….yep…yep…yep… yep! So I mean – all of that – why shouldn't I? That is why I do everything that I do for Mursi. So my life – because of what my mother taught me – is coming full circle with my daughter. She dances, she cheers, and all I do is expose.

Becoming mother. I was about 18 when the doctor said I would probably never have kids. And the things I did to my life in my late teens and my 20s helped fuel that, you know. And one day I made a decision that my life was gonna change. I met God for myself personally and he said: you want to live? (*She nods her head.*) He said, alright. Well I am going to put some things in front of you and it is going to be up to you, but I gotcha. Move forward, I gotcha. I placed everything that you need in front of you. And when I changed my life and went to the doctor, everything that they had been telling me my whole life was gone. And because I had lived so many years thinking I could never have kids, I still was in denial. I did not believe it and I continued to live my life like I could not have kids but in the crevices of my soul I said, "but Lord, I *so* want one" and I would ask Him and question: when?! When my sister had her three kids and *all* my cousins and *everybody* and then one day it was, ooops! I was hooking up with a friend for old times sake – that makes it bad – and [Mursi] asked me about that by the way. She outright came and said "so how did you end up doin it with my daddy?"

Yes ma'am. Yes she did! I said what do you mean? She was like, *do it.* And I asked her, what are you talking about? I said, if you gonna ask a big girl question, ask it the right way. So she said, what made you have sex with my daddy? Girl, you could have bought me for a penny! Woo! So being who I am, I told her the truth (*she lowers her voice almost as if she is trying to whisper*) because I have seen her react to when her father has not given her the whole truth so I don't need her alienated from me for not telling her the truth. I felt she was mature enough to handle it. *Not all of it* but then, that conversation went from laughing to crying because she thought her daddy did not want her, to just realizing that just because a person has a baby doesn't mean they are ready. I was ready. He wasn't.

You know, being a mommy was really easy to me so I um, and also my friend had put the whammy on me (*she is laughing hard!*) She said, you gon get pregnant!

She had seven kids you know, and so my period was late. So the test, I was 37, 36 because I had her when I was 37. I could not even pee on the thing right and it just turned! Girl, I took my mama to the doctor with me and they laughed at me because I had my mama with me at 36 years old – I sure did! The blood test was instantaneous. Girl, I went home and put on maternity clothes! Baby, I owned it from the time that test came back – yes I did! And my pregnancy was, oh it was beautiful. And my favorite song when I was pregnant was "Some Enchanted Evening" by the Temptations. And do you know that is what would make my baby go to sleep? I would listen to that song forever and ohhh I, yeah it was wonderful. I mean I did not get stretch marks or anything!

It starts from the inside when that child is conceived and for me being Mursi's mom started when the test was positive, not when she came. I took on the responsibility of what my mind was thinking while she was on the inside. Because they only had to tell me one time that your child feels everything that you feel. So my first thought was to protect her. I thought "wow." I was carrying her on the inside – I needed to be a certain way. So I surrounded myself with very positive people – positive things – listening to music, going to church, laughing, I watched cartoons, I ate – like, good! I was active – I danced – um – I shopped – everything. So consequently while I was pregnant, she was like baboom baboom baboom ba boom. (*She moves her hands as if she is hitting a drum.*) They said that it was too early for her to move, but at my first ultrasound she flipped her hand and turned her butt up at them and it was like "I'm here so now what?" Yes. Motherhood starts when you realize that test is positive and then you keep that baby.

[You are a] protector because I mean, [the babies] don't know. So you have to guard them against the elements on the outside, even from the doctors and the nurses and stuff like that and I think that is where your prayer life and communicating with the God of your understanding, to guide those doctors and those nurses through just that process, because protection begins – well you know inside. But also when they are on the outside and then from that moment on [you are] teacher because you start teaching them from – well actually I taught her name when I was pregnant. Once I decided on a name, that is what I called her when I was pregnant. So when actually, when she was born and the doctor was like, "oh baby", I was like – her name is Mursi. Call her Mursi. [She was like] "Oh mother" (*she says in a condescending voice*). And I said, no baby you don't understand. White people are not the only ones that talk to their babies while they are pregnant! Call her by her name. I said indulge me – call her. And so sure enough she said "Mursi" and my baby turned her head and looked at her like "what's up?" She knew. She responded to her name from the time she came out because I had talked to her, I had read to her. I danced with her – everything. I talked to her – I rubbed my stomach, I sang to her, you know all that stuff and when she came out, she knew who she was. She knew what her name was. I didn't [know] – I just figured I needed *her* to know and I thought that is what I was supposed to do. You know they give you this whole list of what you should and shouldn't do and I went on what I feel. I didn't [use the list] – I just said I am going to go with what I feel, with what my instincts are, because I always wanted a baby. Always from when I realized I could have kids and when they told me I could not have kids. I said no – and for the longest time that is what I dreamed of.

And family is that unconditional net of love that takes you through the good, the bad and the ugly and when you can come home to a secure and loving place, you are happy. You know you are safe. You know you are loved. No matter what is going on out there you come on and put on your cozy, comfy clothes and go in your girl cave and listen to your music or cut your Wii on and stop downstairs to see your sister who can show you how to walk in heels because your mama done messed up her knees and can't walk in heels anymore. That you can not buy! That's love! That's nurturing. I helped my sister raise her kids. I was always – I always had kids before I got pregnant. My sister's three kids. All of them from the time they were born, or from the time she found out I was pregnant, I have been a part of their lives. Yeah – yeah and I mean on the weekends I would have [Child A]. When [Child B] was a little kid I had her, when [Child C] and [Child D] was born, it was the crew. They all hung out. And then their friends, when we lived in the high-rise, their moms were single moms too. Before Mursi, um – there were probably 8, 9 10, kids somewhere. The oldest, who is 24 now, [List of above mentioned children and more], they can come over and crawl up in my bed or they could you know, spend the night and that kind of thing.

"Old school."   Old school works! But you got to include the new flavor. I remember having a conversation with Mursi one day and she was ragging about going to school and I said, "do you know how many people died to go to school?" I had to break it down. I said people literally died for you to go to school so we can read and not be ashamed for knowing how to read. People died so you could go to any store that you go to today to buy anything that you want to. It was not always like that! You know you can do the old school message… because you would not be here today if these folks had not done it before. (*She pauses and sighs before she resumes.*) You got one life – you got an opportunity. The one thing that you can do that nobody can take away from you is get your education! And be a responsible, productive member of society. Be responsible for yourself. Own up to what you do. If you did wrong, be woman enough to say: I made a mistake. Own who you are and what you do. And dream. If you dream and you see it, you can do it. You got to work hard for it. Nothing in this world is free. All of that is how our parents raised us. All of that still holds true today.

The world that we live in today is not Black and White – it ain't even Black, White, and Gray. It is multicolored, all shapes, sizes, culture, nature – everything and if you don't expose them to that – they will grow up thinking it is one certain way and that hinders their coping skills. If you don't expose them to White people or deal with Hispanic, or Indian, or Asian people, when they get out into the workforce, they are not going to be able to handle that. So do I want to hinder my child like that? No! Your exposure has a level of responsibility to it. You have to guide them through the exposure – you don't just set them out there and let them loose – you walk with them and you answer their questions and you show them this, and you show them that and you talk about this and you talk about that and a couple of her teachers – we were talking after this first marking period – [are] exposing them to world and current events. Getting the *New York Times* for the kids. Letting them read and knowing what is happening with Khadafi because that is the world. That strengthens their vocabulary. That strengthens them as a person and you never know the gifts that are inside a person if you don't show them things. They will never get the opportunity to realize some gifts if you don't expose them. How will they know if they are a dancer or a politician or a lawyer or an architect or a bus driver? Or a garbage person or a, um an IT person or a scientist – all of those things our kids can be, or a fashion designer.

[I am her] teacher – authority figure, and I think there are more roles to evolve as she gets older. I would love one day for her to be able to say that I am one of her closest friends. I did not have that with my mom – she was very old school: I am never going to be your friend – I am always going to be your mother. And right now – in order to be an effective authority figure and in order to be her mom – I can not be her friend because friends are going to let you get away with things and friends are going to co-sign your crap and I just, I just can't do that. I just – I believe when you plant the seeds and you water, then they grow. If you start them out as little bitty babies raising them ain't all that bad. The challenges are going to come – Yes! Girlfriend can hit that last nerve and I tell her, "girlfriend, don't take your own life in your own hands like that." Or sometimes I say, "girl do you know Jesus just saved your life?" Mursi was raised on the look. And sometimes, that's all it has to be. But at some point as she gets older and becomes an even more responsible adult and lives her life and when she begins to go through love and meet her husband and have my grandbaby or grandbabies, I want to be a nurturing friend. I want to take that to the next level that I did not have with my mom. From my mom, I learned to give my child what she gave me and more. That is the cornerstone of who I am as Mursi's mom.

Leadership.   Starting with home – well starting with herself – her body, her mind, her spirit – she is not learning if I am not teaching her to take care of her body. How can she ever grow up and take care of somebody? Going through her menstrual period – all of those things. Dealing with her self-esteem, owning who she is right where she is at – not sweating it. And teaching her responsibility with the home. One of the things that we are doing more and more, she is taking more of an active role with me and budgeting finances. No, we can't always go shop, we have bills to pay. "Well, what's the bills?" The light, the gas, the alarm, the internet, the phones. Our toiletries, our groceries, your bus service, your dance tuition, toe shoes all of those things. You need clothes because you can't wear what you wore last winter – so we need some things. And for a minute she was talking about the money, the money, the money. And I said, back up! It ain't about the money, it is about responsibility. So, you know she has taken a more active role in that and I give her a chunk of money for her chores and stuff like that. And she has to buy the little things, the little knick-knack things that she likes, like her nail polish and stuff. She has to put a certain amount of money in the church; I leave that to her discretion and if I don't feel it is appropriate I say, "really?" Because that is a part of your service to God. Because you are always asking for things and so what are you doing for Him? And washing clothes, keeping her room clean. As a matter of fact come and let me show you – this is all her. I actually had it painted before we actually moved in. *She takes me on a tour of Mursi's "girl cave" with posters of Justin Bieber and Jaden Smith on the purple walls, dozens of books, girl toys I remember from my own childhood, and a Minnie Mouse television.*

Now iTunes girlfriend, she is going to get into! She manages her iTunes account well. I give her a certain amount of money and I don't say you have to keep this within a certain amount of time, but because she loves her music and she wants to put it on her iPod, she knows those songs have to be censored through me. She just can't go onto iTunes and get whatever she wants because she ain't grown. We have a discussion – and now I have to listen to this music! (*She sighs, smiles and throws her head to the side.*) It was um, Kanye West's song – I can't stand Kanye West! But some song that he was talking about his struggles with his daughter and not being able to be in her life and going through all of that and I thought really... So I can let her listen to that song because it talks about a life struggle. Also Lil Wayne, "How to Love" is on point. It talks about coping with your lack of self-esteem and the choices that you make and what you are willing to settle for. Now what are you going to do? She introduced me to that song with Lil Wayne – she is listening to the *words*. So I got to quit: stop being so strict and listen. And it is humbling. And it is so rewarding to listen to my kid. It brings me to tears sometimes because if you listen, you will see their growth. And you can appreciate their personality as they are growing and her accepting responsibility when she falls short and getting her to admit when she is not making good choices. *Later in the conversation, Maya's phone rings and the Lil Wayne song plays. I completely raise my eyebrows and ask is that in fact her phone. She says,* Girl, look, I'm comin up in the world!

I have always said to Mursi since she said she wanted to be a new creature in Christ – she wanted to be baptized – this is what that means. You are called to be different – I don't care what your friends do. I emphatically put my foot down because when she gets in her way, she gets in her way. [I tell her] you are an 8th grader (*she claps her hands loudly*). Act like it! Because although she is in 7th now, my mentality of pushing her is – no, you are in 8th grade because you want to transfer out of this school and go to an academy. You can not transfer out and go to an academy acting like a 7th grader. Sister, you have to rock 8th grade when you walk in the door.

[Preparing] and protecting Mursi means having honest and real conversations. Not cutting off the news and letting her see. As hard as that is – that is the world that we live in so. Reality enforces when we have a plan if you are supposed to go from point A to point B and we have a plan as to how you are supposed to get to point A and point B. Your safety depends on you doing exactly what we have always been doing. When you deviate, these are the things that can happen. Like with the guy being killed outside our front lawn. When we came home, we got our stuff together and we came directly into the house. Trouble can't get here unless you open the door and let it in! So consequently – for me – [protecting] is just being honest, being gut-wrenchingly honest. You have to pay attention to her surroundings. Allowing her to catch the CTA.[3] She has done it once. *She has only done it once!* But she did it. By herself from her school to my job! We have caught the bus before, but allowing her to do it by herself and her feeling comfortable with that and going through different scenarios. So if the bus is crowded, this is what you need to do. Or when standing at the bus stop, we need to be talking so somebody knows where you are at or what you are doing. When you get on the bus, make sure you stay close to the bus driver so the bus driver can see if anything is happening with you. When you get ready for your stop, don't be sitting on the phone texting, pay attention. Having those kinds of conversations with her. When we are out, don't be talking on the phone when you are walking with me – nuh uh – put that phone up! You know, pay attention to your surroundings. And teaching her how to drive so when the time comes she knows how. [She is] 12 but she is tall enough to reach the pedals! We just, if anything were to happen and she is in the car with me, I don't need her freaking out! I have to look at how I prepare her for life events. She is going to freak out, but she. can. handle. it. (*she claps her hands to emphasize every word*) because I have given her some tools to use. I have exposed her to difficult things.

A mother is a mother – a mommy, and you either going to raise your kid like you are supposed to or you ain't. I have never been boxed in. There probably are [stereotypes associated with Black mothers] but that is not something that I look at or care anything about because my mother did not raise me like that. You know, they're out there and I see them and I know them, but does that define me? Absolutely not because you put your panties on one leg at a time just like I do. You pull your bra up the same way that I do. (*She pauses for a while and then speaks again breaking the silence as if I have provoked her in some way.*) And you know what? I hear a lot of people talk about that and it irritates the crap out of me. Because I have a couple of friends that say the Europeans this, the Europeans that....grrr! We have no excuses. You choose to be a responsible, productive member. How responsible you are is up to you. When I see [discrimination], it does irritate me but it pushes me to do more. There is money out there to be made. The question is, are you going to present yourself, not as a Black person, as a person? Are you going to position yourself to get that money? Now, yes, as a Black person I am going to probably have to work harder. I am going to have to endure a lot more crap, but my thought is that Jesus endured so much – who am I? That irritates me and that pushes me to set myself apart because I see that what God has given me is for me and I am supposed to shine. I am not supposed to be like this – I am not supposed to be passive. As I get older yes, there are times where... silence is golden. My mother always said: never let everybody know what you know. Because one day everything that you know – I promise you – all you got to do is bring the [record of your performance] down and say bam! Let your work speak.

NIKKI

I immediately perceived her as the businesswoman of the group. I liked Nikki the first time I saw her, but I found her to be a bit intimidating. On an early Saturday morning, she was pretty 'put-together' with makeup, hair, and attire, even in a casual way. She spoke fast and proper with a full voice and struck me as solid middle-class. Her profession came up a couple of times so that I figured her to also be one of the mothers the school staff felt was 'safe' or rather, non-threatening: She was very articulate, action-oriented, light-skinned, and I seem to remember her having substantial rock on her left ring finger. In the meeting, she spoke less of her son – Nkrumah – and more about the administrative duties of the parent organization. She has a board position – having a critical influence upon administration and decision-making for the school. I got the sense that she was operating as if she were at work; however, the longer the meeting, the more relaxed her tongue. I was excited when she, Maya, and Sonia invited me to lunch, along with two of the children, after one of our meetings. We had a brief personal conversation and discovered a couple of parallels in our lives.

When I first contacted her to begin our interviews, she was incredibly receptive and assured me that "the door was open" for whatever I needed. Because of schedule conflicts, we only had one interview, which was during the second round. She welcomed me into her home the way I imagined a big sister would. This was the first time I met her son, Nkrumah. I found it awesome that one his friends came over for a sleepover and he arrived with a Lego suitcase in hand – mainly because it reminded me of how I used to play with my friends and it evoked feelings of innocence and pure enjoyment. There were occasions during the interview that Nkrumah popped in and out to ask permission for something – either about food or games he wanted to play. Throughout our 2-hour interview, Nikki makes many references to being perceived as "soft" – which she largely attributes to being biracial.[4] This is critical in how she exercises her voice, privilege, and messages for her son.

Learning mother. My mother was everything to me. She could fix anything, she could do everything right. I think when I got to high school that she was going through her own thing. Being the age that I am now, I completely understand it. But I felt resentful in a lot of ways or that she was not there for me. And I must say both of my sisters were teen mothers so I was the youngest child up until the time I was 12. My niece was born when my sister was – she was 14 when she got pregnant and 15 when she had her daughter. So I think from like 12 on up I just felt like on my own, taking care of what I needed to do. You know I lived in the suburbs, I did not live in the city or ride on the CTA. I don't want to give you that impression. But you

53

know, I was on the volleyball team and my mother wasn't there. She had to work and I had to find a way home. But I was also very independent in terms of like, I started doing teenage things when I was younger because it was always like, "take your sister with you." So I was 12 years old drinking Southern Comfort with teenage kids that I should not have been with. But I think what that taught me was to make some better decisions for myself because no one else was making these decisions for me. Um, so you know, in high school, I did not have a – what do you call it – when you have to be home? (*Nikki is struggling to find the word 'curfew'*.) Yeah, one time my mom tried to pull it. She felt like she had been soft on my sisters, and they went in that (*she gestures away from herself*) direction. I think most of my life and family experiences being the youngest child and the child that had the least choice in the family, I think I've grown up to the be the most outspoken. But I would say what [my mother] taught me was more valuable than anything else, which was common sense. Like I said, even though I did not have a curfew, I would be like, "yall I am ready to go in the house, I know yall don't have to be in until 1:00, but phishhh, but I'm tired." I think that is why I survived college. I think that is why I was able to make those decisions for myself. (*She takes a long pause and begins to talk as if she is still thinking*) I have never had this question asked of me – "what did my mother teach me?" I think it was much easier to love my mother when I realized she was not a superwoman. When I realized that she could *not* fix everything and she did not have every single answer. That is when I started to really appreciate her. But, I also had those, you know, you still have those resentments and it's like – it is what it is.

Now, I feel a little too responsible for being that superwoman and being able to do everything [in the] image of the successful Black mother, because we are all single, you know what I am saying? I think there is a certain sense of having to be on top of it all the time. Like I am in [the grocery store] tonight on the phone trying to get an ad in because my colleague called me and said this woman is all freaking out. I said, I will call her right now. So, I am in the checkout line but it is not a big deal. And at the end of the day I am like, Jesus I am tired. And I think that is kind of where I fail SSCES because I feel a certain sense of responsibility for the Beacons not kind of keeping that momentum. But at the same time I have to say, at the end of the day I go to work early, girl, and I will still be working when *you* leave tonight. So it is... I need the support as well but I feel I should *be* the support, so why am I *asking* for the support?

Becoming mother. I didn't make that choice. (*She laughs loud.*) I mean, you know I was 24, um – I had been broken up with his dad for a month and a half. Yeah, and was like, um where is my period? I was pregnant and was abortion an option? Of course it was. Other things were an option, but at the time I felt like for me, I had my college degree – I was going back for my Masters – but I have my degree, I know I can do this. So I made the choice simply because I felt like at that time, that was the right choice for me. I knew that his father and I were not going to get back together and that the road ahead was going to be a tough one. And it has been one in terms of our relationship. I don't get no child support – I don't get any support what so ever. But Nkrumah has *two* fathers. So I have my ex- boyfriend. We were together ten years – from the time Nkrumah was 2 – until two months ago. He is going to take him next weekend. That's his father and he knows his role. That's his father and is his male model. That is who he looks to, that is who he acts like, that is who his mannerisms come from and I think his biological father is well aware of that. He does see his biological father – I have made that a priority. I have a hundred thousand miles on my car [getting him back and forth to his father]. I do have to say that I have tried to help him. I have tried to advise him on going back to trade schools and done what I can even in a space where I can't stand him. (*She chuckles.*) This is Nkrumah's father. So even though he is not the best, Nkrumah deserves a healthy, okay father. Um, but he also knows how his father is. And he is very aware.

"Mother to son".[5]   We have talked about STD's. We have talked about masturbation. We have talked about – I don't want grandbabies by a hood rat. You know what I mean, for real. So you need to know what chlamydia looks like, you need to know HIV looks like. You need to know what herpes looks like – it is nasty! You know what I mean? We have to just put it out there. He always comes to me and says, can I just ask you for some advice real quick? He will get advice about a girl. He is very – very open.

This morning he asked me about Penn State. Yeah, it was on… we watch WGN every morning because they are hilarious and they were covering Penn State and he asked, "what is this? What is going on? I have seen a lot of this lately," and I told him exactly what the situation was. I said that – that Coach Sandusky – he took boys about your age – that looked just like you – into a locker room and had sex with them anally, you know in their behind. Mortified face, right? But you see those kids that are protesting? And he said, "yea." They are protesting for [Joseph Paterno] to stay. They are supporting him. And that – he did not even look horrified. He was speechless. He could not understand. And so I guess my point is that I feel like I am preparing him for our – our society values system. We value football over protecting our children being abused. And um, you need to know that and you need to understand the world that we are coming into and we just have – I mean, I just try to have real conversations with him that are going to benefit him in life. And every day I ask myself, am I telling my child too much? I don't know. And I don't think none of us really know unless you have studied mothering and unless you have had many kids and stuff. But for a lot of us, it is just kind of doing it as I go.

There was an instance about him bullying one of his friends over an empty seat in art class. [I asked Nkrumah] if you know that [your friend] has emotions that get a hold of him and gets upset about little things like that – if it is just a seat, why couldn't you give it up? And he had a hard time answering that question. Well, I am going to tell you why I think you did it and you are going to tell me if I am right or if I am wrong. And if I am wrong, I am wrong. I think that you would not have done that to [she lists names], I named kids in his class that I knew were a little bit hard.

I think that you did that to [this friend] because you felt you could get away with doing that to [him]. What do you think about that? And he said, you're right, that is why I did that. And I said to him, "Nkrumah, I think that I am raising you to fight for the weaker person and not identify their weaknesses and take advantage of them."

I feel like that kind of tells a story about how we are in my house in terms of talking about what is happening at Penn State or what is happening in whatever realm. I just feel like I am trying to raise him as a conscious person and conscious of what is happening around him. Part of that is because he so does not pay attention. But we are also trying to understand each other. And I want to show you an article – this is my child, he (*Nikki interrupts herself to grab a parenting magazine from the kitchen bar*) – I have done a lot of yelling lately because I have been frustrated with him not listening. One thing that drove me crazy Billye, oh my God, is, there is a ritual: You go in the bathroom, you brush your teeth, you wash your face, you *put lotion on your face,* you brush your hair and you put some grease in it. I mean there are all these things that we have had to go through and the other day I kissed him on the cheek and could tell he did not put lotion on and lost it! I lost it because I was just like, AHH! – I don't ask you to take out the garbage, do dishes. Just put some lotion on! So it is things like that. So I had to stay at the school late one night and he was in the principal's office reading through this magazine and he literally pointed out this article that he would like me to read. He said, "ma – ma, page 103, I want you to read this article." (*She hands the magazine to me and flips to an article titled, "Are you listening to me?"*) And at first I thought that it was him saying (*she laughs*) "bitch, are you listening to me?" And I'm like, oh my God! – oh my God, I am horrible. (*We are both laughing.*) No, but we are actually going to read it together. I was like, have you read it? He said he read some of it. I said, well you need to read it too if you are going to refer that to me. You need to know what it says. So we are going to read it together this weekend because actually his next [school] essay is going to be on that article.

Deconstructing Blackness. I did not know I was Black until I went to college. I knew I was mixed… but… yeah when I took that African-American History course, I think that's when my eyes were open for the first time and I was like – I am a Black person. Regardless of the green eyes that I see in the mirror and the pale skin and this hair, I am a Black woman. And for years when I would go with my dad somewhere on Michigan Avenue, we would be stared at or we would have been followed. I never [understood] that; it did not register for me. I think that my experience [as] a half Black, half White person in this country is completely unique.

So like with Nkrumah. My child has never gotten a write up before so this has been the first teacher that has called me. I was like "are you sure you are calling the right Nikki, mother of Nkrumah, are you sure you are calling me – me right?" And she was like "yeah," she was not amused. (*Nikki and I are both laughing.*) This incident involved him kind of being pestered by a friend of his – a good friend. And he said to his friend um, if you don't leave me alone I am going to kill you. So that was a major referral. Because that is violent language. And that is language that I try to limit. He loves video games. He loves Xbox. He likes the violent stuff. But we talk about that. This stuff is not real and if he were to go over to Iraq or Afghanistan, this would not be the situation. [He has] got to understand that. But my ex and I had to sit him down that night and tell him what his words mean. There is power in your voice. And pretty soon you are going to be 16 years old and 6'4" and they are not going to know you still have hug time with your mama, or that your mama has to remind you to zip up your pants in the morning. They are going to see you as a 6'4" young man and you are going to have to have a cool head about you. You are going to have to see that your words matter and these are all of our conversations since he started 7th grade. We have had so many of these conversations about what is to grow up, what it is to be a Black male.[6] I can only speak to a certain, you know, perspective of that. But I am lucky to have a male role model for him that can give him examples of when he has been questioned by police and when he knew that he didn't do anything wrong [except that] he 'fit the description.' You always have to be cool. You have to be on the level that you know you did not do any wrong. But you can't use language like that because people are going to look at you very different. Even different from the White boy language. It just comes out differently and you are a threat. So it has been difficult to have these conversations with him because it is a reminder that he is growing up and I am really preparing him to be out in the world. But they are necessary and they have to be had.

Nkrumah asked me, "why these kids call me White boy?" and I was like because you are light-skinned and that is just what they say. You are gonna have to let it roll off you. You know that you are not White and because he is working on fractions right now, we went through the whole, half, an octoroon, and a quadroon (*we are both amused by this*) and we had this whole discussion. And so I have always been very up front about that. He knows that the reason that his name is Nkrumah is because I knew he was going to look like that: I knew he was going to be a little light-skinned, pretty little curly-haired boy and so – I [originally] wanted to name him Christian. But I knew in my heart of hearts that I could not have a light-skinned boy named Chris. So, His name is Nkrumah Christian [surname] – and I knew that I needed a strong name for him because he was going to look the way that he does. *And* I know how folks look at resumes and I made it so that if he wanted to do "N. Christian [surname]" he could do that on his resume. Giiirl, I gave WAY too much thought to it I'm sure, but I felt like I had to because he can't be considered soft – soft boy Chris – he can't.

And we've talked about the perceptions and why in the Black community there is still this intra-cultural racism. But outside of this, there is racism that is pointed directly at us, so we have just had conversations from a very historical perspective cause I am just a logical person. Because when I was little I was – I am beige because my father is brown and my mother is crème colored – so BAM! – this is the color of my skin. My eyes are this color because my mama has blue eyes and he got brown eyes and I have this gold and green thing, you know? For me it was logical. So I think my approach with him is the very same way that, you know, you are going to be viewed *this* way in the Black community and you are going to be viewed *this* way by the rest of the world. And in the Black community you are going to be a soft, light-skinned boy and they are going to test you and in the world at large you are going to be a Black man. It is the duality like DuBois[7] discusses.

So we just talk about the roles that we have to play – the fact that I have to play different roles in different spaces. I have to be a different person to different people. For example, in my company, we are going to meet with – I don't know – a multi-cultural prospect and they are going to take me. *I know why you are taking me.* It is like the whole Obama thing when White folks want to claim him, "oh he is not all Black," but he really *is* Black in your eyes. He is Black in society. I feel like we are really getting off track, but I also feel that, um, I feel that I get a little bit more respect in the school because of that. That bugs me and I hate to say that out loud but I see that. But I will play that role and if my role at SSCES is to be this safe light-skinned lady who can relate to us (*referring to the Black faculty and staff*), then I will be that too. So I just tend to play the role that the situation requires and I am trying to teach him the same thing. I have never been a big fighter, but I have always felt physically like folks think one way about me because of the way that I look. And I know my mouth. So I have to be prepared for what's gonna happen after I open my mouth and we get into the bottom of things.

I tend not to worry so much about how other people perceive me as a Black mother because my own expectations are to not fail. Because I feel that is the perception of most people – that we will fail. So that is what makes me be on the Board, and that is what makes me mentor on Saturday mornings. I feel it is my responsibility to the community. You know I have a son, but we have a lot of Black girls that need a lot of help. So Saturday mornings, I mentor with [name of organization], which is sort of my way of giving to the girls. It is all about communication and we talk about how to present yourself because we need children to be successful and they are not going to be successful if people are always cussing each other out and this and that. And I feel I have a certain responsibility because of that. And I feel a certain sense of guilt because of knowing better, like I need to be the one to tell you how it is and help you out. So I sometimes feel like I have that martyr savior complex, but at the same time I genuinely care and genuinely enjoy my time with the girls and helping them, and modeling for them and just answering questions and being open with them.

School choices. I [have a mutual friend] that works at CPS so she emailed me a list of schools I could look at – a lot of new charter schools and SSCES was one. It is an extended school day, which I really loved, which is one of the things when I would volunteer, I was literally running with the teacher because the whole day was like rush, rush, rush. So people who were like 8 – 4? That is so long! It is not. Try going to a 8:30 – 1:30 school. They have time for *nothing*. They are rushing through everything. So long story short, I went up to SSCES the very last day because I got the list a little late and they were doing orientation. [The first principal of the school][8] was there and she was like literally packing up and putting things in boxes. I remember it was raining and I was like, I am so sorry and parents were gone. But she sat there and talked to me for like 90 minutes. And we discovered how much commonality we had: I was a historian, I had worked at the DuSable [African-American History] Museum and she is the great-niece of a legendary curator. So that kicked it off and we were just like blah, blah, blah.

School relationships.   So I think that I bring resources [to SSCES] in terms of being a safe parent that can be talked to in a high-level way and understand it and carry that message – I hate to do that – but you understand what I am trying to say. To carry that message to the broader school community and I have given [the school] a lot of feedback. There is a certain level of respect that I get there, but I also feel that they know I am on their side and they talk to me. I have had a number of teachers say to me I am dying here – I am tired, I am worn out, we can't have meaningful conversations because I feel like I am afraid that someone is going to walk into the classroom and see we are not focused on testing – a whole other issue, but I feel that teachers trust me – both Black and White. I am that safe space.

I have gotten a lot of weird faces, but you know you have to frame how to talk to Black people. You have to think about how you talk to people about their children. You have to understand when you tell Black folk, and especially a single Black woman: "oh by the way, this year, every other Friday we have a 2:00 dismissal." That's very different. You have to frame that for parents. You have to present it in a way that is not intimidating, because change normally means something bad is coming. And so when you switch out a teacher, *no* it is not just switching out a teacher. No, you need to address that with these parents because they have trusted *this* White woman. And another White woman coming in here that they don't know? You have to frame that in a whole different way.

And I am trying to work with the [new] principal because she is a White woman from the South. You know she is young and she is struggling and I emailed her the other day and was like, dude if you need to vent – I am there. I am a Board member, but understand that I am a human first and foremost and I can just listen to you and try to help you and try to prioritize and help you figure these things out but you have to tell me how things are. But I think my biggest resource for the school honestly is just being an honest voice that says, you are doing this really shitty. That is insane that you are not thinking about how you are communicating to these parents. That is like the first step – like in saying the right things and framing your messages in the right way that they are going to be received positively. You can't just say to folks, "yep every other Friday it is going to be 2 o'clock [dismissal] – peace" because people are like – dude I work at Currency Exchange and I don't get to leave. And I am a consultant and right now *I* am freaking out because I am leaving every day at 3:30 because [my ex] moved out and I don't have that same support for pick up and drop off. So you know I come home and he does homework and I continue working and I make sure I email my boss and say I am working… Um, and as much of a pain in the butt it is to be on the phone with that woman in Portland trying to get this ad in the newspaper, that is still a luxury when you look at how work is for people and you look at what their demands are. It is still a luxury that I can take care of my job and do grocery shopping – even as much as I don't like it. You have people that just have to sit at Currency Exchange until 6 o'clock, 8 o'clock. They can't get off at 1:30 to come get their child, so it is relative. You know what I'm saying? And now (*redirecting her conversation to the principal again*) it is messed up – how you just delivered this message and we have to figure out how to do it better next time. And I get the whole – okay – I mean you are uncomfortable, and I am a little uncomfortable too, but it is a conversation that needs to be had. So I, I think that has been my biggest contribution, but I would like to see other contributions. For me, time is my enemy. I mean literally it has just been time and being able to commit to [being involved at the school].

I do a lot of these discipline hearings because I do feel that it is so important for these White teachers to understand what misbehaving looks like in the Black community and if a little Black girl sucks her teeth, that [should not warrant] a write up. And you need to be able to overlook that. And at some point she has to stop, but in 4th grade she sucked her teeth, whatever – get over it. When she calls you a bitch – *then talk to me.* You know what I'm saying? You have to learn what the levels are and you have to understand our culture. So I sit in these hearings because the majority of our Board is White and I feel that there needs to be communication and there needs to be – I mean I am the middle. I have been a fence rider my whole life, I have had teachers write that on paper: "You are a fence rider. Pick a side" – and I am like no. I am going to see the sides that need to be seen and I am going to assign relevance to them and I am going to choose the side that to me makes the most sense. I am always going to see both sides because I have no choice other than to do that... I am gray.

CAROLYN

Carolyn is the woman that nearly every SSCES mother points to as a support. She is seemingly the backbone of the organization because she is the initial contact for all parents in the school. She is regarded as "the reason my child is here," and "the reason I am active as a parent." She smiles, never really taking credit for the praise given to her by the parents and will sometimes have tears in her eyes when she speaks passionately. The parents feel comfortable talking with her openly. Carolyn also has a child enrolled in this school, so she plays the dual role of administrator and parent. You can tell she carries the responsibility of being honest with her parents about the frustrations she feels from both sides. She often 'puts a bubble in her mouth' (which literally looks like her puffing her cheeks out to hold her tongue and provide slight amusement), takes notes, nods her head, and speaks very patiently.

I worked with Carolyn the most – three days of every week. If we were not in physical contact, we were emailing or phoning. Our relationship was certainly strained in the beginning; I was brought in as an outside contractor to formalize and execute a project she'd already been independently operating. It was clear that my position was a slap in the face. To add injury to insult, I was to work directly with her, in her office, and develop additional projects for her to execute, on top of the two roles she had already been assigned. She had also just been passed over for the position of principal months before I arrived. She never verbally communicated her frustration to me but through her patient smiles and constant moving to keep with her responsibilities, it was obvious on many occasions. For these reasons, I deferred to her often and stepped up to assist her. I kept constant, open communication, careful not to come across as her babysitter or spy, as I had to maintain communication with her supervisors reporting of my progress and how she was assisting me. She was leaps and bounds ahead of me with experience, not only as an administrator but the mother of two pre/teenaged daughters – Kanuri and Khoi. Yet, I was assigned as a peer of some sort – I had to trust her. And if neither one of us wanted to feel like I was simply getting in the way or making more work for her, she had to trust me as well. Additionally, not only was I responsible for developing a parent incentive program (which was slowly taking shape before I arrived), I was assisting with school administrative duties – specifically school enrollment (which is very critical in an urban "school of choice").

Before long, the focus became less about the job – that was pretty routine and we avoided stepping on one another's toes – and more about Carolyn being a mother, wife, and lover of House music. As she began to warm up to me, several other members of the staff engaged with me as well. Many of them were family members through blood and marriage, so their connection was very intimate and supportive; they provided a relaxed energy on many tense days. Soon I was invited to her home and began a relationship with her daughters. She is fiercely protective; therefore, I was honored when she allowed her oldest daughter to attend a late evening poetry event. Of all the parents I have worked with, Carolyn is the one with whom I was most intimately involved. I have interacted with members of her immediate family and she has been supportive of both my partner and I in events outside of our primary relationship. Due to schedule conflicts, we were only able to have one interview, which lasted approximately one hour and took place after work at a restaurant on the South Side. We were joined by Khoi.

Involved mother. My mother wanted to make sure that we got something more; we weren't gonna be the status quo. She advocated. She pushed to make sure that we got the best education we could possibly get and we knew that we had to go to college. We knew that. That was at the top of her list because that was something she was not able to achieve. She went to junior college for about a year and that was it. So it was not an option to not go to college. [She made] sure that I had everything that I needed – from school supplies to tutors to transportation to – all across the board. I did not miss any events. When I was in high school, starting my freshmen year, I went into the Upward Bound program for all 4 years. She just made sure that I was always doing something positive.

Back then it was not a lot of parent involvement. I only remember [my mother coming] report card conference time, report card pickup. And then any school event, like if there was a show or performance or parent meeting, she was always there. And then I had a relative in the school too. It was like she was just there. There was no getting in trouble. So [my brother and I] always had to make good choices. It wasn't like, I'm gonna act the fool because I can. It just did not happen because she was that stern: these are my expectations, this is what you are going to do and that's *it*. She wasn't mean, we just did not want to disappoint her – so we didn't.

When I became a parent, it completely changed what I wanted to do with my life – completely. I never grew up thinking I was gonna be a teacher or in education – that is not something that I wanted to do. But when I became a parent that kind of superseded everything and um – I decided all my focus and energy would go towards them and that is what it has been. And still is.

School choices. I was the director of a day care center and through the mail I received a flyer about a new charter school – SSCES. I liked that it was a new school and that it offered parents a choice. Um, I loved the structure of the school and that it was college focused and they were doing something different. I felt like I had a voice. Like Khoi was *not* – I didn't want her to go to a traditional Chicago school. Unfortunately, I did not live in the best neighborhood at the time so sending her to her neighborhood school was never an option. It was *never* an option. Because I had been – I had not only worked in Chicago Public Schools, but I had been – I had seen administration, I had seen other PTAs or PTCOs[9] as they call them and just did not like the way things were being done. How they managed the school, how they managed the children, um – and it was just not something that I wanted for [Khoi or Kanuri]. So, it was either find a charter school or something private. Those were my choices, those were my options.

It was the arts infusion piece [of SSCES] that kind of drew me in. That is Khoi's love and what is she completely focused on. I thought it would be a great fit for her – not for me, but for her. She enjoys music, art, dance, drawing – so I was like let me see what this is about and when I went to the open house I was talking to the principal and she was just taken aback by my interest in the school. She asked what did I do and I told her and she was like "oh you need to come here and work…"

School relationships. My expectations [of the teachers] are that they believe in and are passionate about what they do or what they say that they were going to do once being a part of, you know, our children's educational endeavors. This is not something that we take lightly and so when I sit on the interview panel, I don't just look at you educational wise and what your background is, I want to see your passion. Like, is this something that you are really passionate about? Are you going to do your best to develop a relationship with your students and their parents, and is this something that you really want to do? Because this is not just about teaching – it is far more beyond that – and if it is not there, it is going to show.

Having a relationship with the parents, is something that I think everybody should have – not just me. That is why I have the least problem with the parents [at SSCES] because they know me and I know them and it is as simple as that. It is not rocket science. I am not doing anything special – hanging out with them – nothing extra. It is just I have taken the time to make this my priority – to get to know them because they trust me with their child. And I want you to know exactly what I'm here for. When I call parents about discipline, I get no push back: "I trust you. My child was acting up. Do what you have to do. I apologize so…"

I care. The board noticed that there was a deficit with parent involvement, not because of the tone but because of the data. Data, data, data – the attendance at parent meetings, the [school issued] surveys about parent satisfaction. So um – this past summer they sent myself and another young lady to a [professional development] to find out about this new parent involvement program called *I Care*. It's called, *I Care Parent Involvement*. Excellent program – difficult to implement. They say it is easy and when we went to the training we were like oh we can do this, we can do this. But to get parents to buy into it, it is hard. So the goal is, their whole mindset is, parent involvement is not just coming into the building. It is what you are doing with your child at home, the whole nine. So at the beginning of the month a form goes home to the parents: This is the characteristic. (*A characteristic would be something like 'kindness' or 'sharing'.*) There is an activity you can do and we want you to share what *you're* doing. [Additionally] in the classroom, the teacher is teaching a lesson on the same characteristic. Then at the end of the month the teacher sends home a feedback form so we can *see* and this is your opportunity to document what you have done. So we see it's starting to open the dialogue to see what the differences are – what you are doing. If students that don't ordinarily get compliments, get them or get praised. Because [the parents] send those forms back and then the teachers get to talk to the kids about it or whatever, but you get to *see*. And then we put this information into a data system and it is supposed to, hopefully it is supposed to curb our behavior. But we just started [last month].

And of course this is something that I had to do, again, because I am a parent. Which I found very difficult to do. And the only reason that I did it was because I had to do it. But once I did it – it was great. What was difficult was finding the time to do the assignment, to do the project. Even thought I had *30 days*. So you had 30 days to do this assignment and it could be nothing big. It could be reading a book with your child, it could be going to the park, to the movies. But ours was middle school – more of having conversations. So we had to have conversations about being a good listener, what that looks like, what it sounds like, what it feels like… I found out that

63

I was not listening to her as much as I should have been. Through the discussion we just found out more things about each other and *we do* spend a lot of time together and *we do* talk a lot but I guess you know, as a parent you always miss some things. It just made us just stop and think.

Something she brought to my attention before when I was talking about transferring her, she said to me: "Like, if you feel like I am not learning everything I need to learn, why don't you just give me what I'm missing?" You have a point. And so I started doing it and now every week we have a vocabulary word on the refrigerator and she has to add a sentence to it. Everybody gets to contribute – and this helped her. These are words that I encourage her to use in school and so this is something that I would not have thought to do on my own, I probably would have but that I had to do it…

[*I Care*] is definitely supportive. Because it gives you activities but there is also room for you to make lists. And so we did a couple of the activities but I feel it opened up the dialogue like – for example – I am always refereeing something between her and her sister but understanding that they listen to each other differently. We figured out for instance, that I do not like to communicate in the morning, none of us do, but we force ourselves to say good morning when we don't want to instead of respecting each others' space and respecting who we are and what we like. So, just talking about it and implementing it has been interesting.

JILL

When we first met, she was pregnant with her second daughter. Jill was always present for our meetings but not someone who caught my immediate attention; she was more of a quiet force. She was not one of the initial parents that I contacted but Carolyn strongly suggested that I should. What I found through our interview was that she is a teacher and balances the responsibilities of motherhood with the perceptions and expectations of school administrators, of which she is intimately familiar. What was most interesting about her is that her roles as mother and teacher are closely intertwined. We spoke a lot about expectations and discipline and it was many times indistinguishable which role was impacting her ideas and choices. More than once she described herself as "non-confrontational" however, when she spoke either of her daughter Jola, or her students, her tone was strong and certain.

Unlike the other mothers, the most time I spent with Jill was during this interview. What makes her important to this project are the ways she stands out from the other mothers. Not only is she the only one employed as a CPS classroom teacher, but she is also the only one who was married when I met her (still is), not originally from Chicago, and the only one with a private/boarding school background. Our interview took place during the first round. Therefore, we focused quite a bit on school structure; her frustrations as a teacher; her expectations for Jola; the I Care program; and how she balanced all of her roles with the addition of a new baby. Jill agreed to meet me at the South Side Starbucks. It was a beautiful day and we talked for about an hour and a half on the outdoor patio.

Involved mother.   I think my experience [as a student] was – we want you to pay your tuition, we got the rest of this! To me it was like, what [the parent needs] to do is make sure your kid has lunch, or their uniform, but I don't recall there being a lot of outreach about this is what you should do with your kid at home. Because you are paying this money, we are going to make sure you are getting the education that you are paying for. So you can learn another language and all that kind of rich stuff that you want – that all kids deserve. All kids deserve to learn another language.

I think over time, parent involvement has become a higher expectation for schools. Schools have more outreach, more programs for that, I think. So at SSCES, I feel the outreach more because they have this *I Care*. Their theme last month was creativity. So when we got it, they said these are the suggestions: take your child to the library and get your child a library card and do this, and do this. They are telling us what to do with our kid, right? So at first I was like, my kid has had a library card since she was you know, like 4 years old and I was like who are they to tell me – like assume that I don't know? I talked to some people at my school where I work and one of the teachers was saying that we had parents that didn't know that that is what they should do. Or, had not thought about that is what they should do. So I took a step back and said I just can't take it personally. And then they sent home this paper at the end of the month that we have to turn in. You have to write five things that you did with your kid this month that has something to do with creativity and I was like, oh one more thing!

I started to push the thing off again and then I was thinking well, I try to teach Jola that sometimes you got to do things you don't want to do. And so I was sitting there thinking – well we did this – I let her style her hair one day. Just little stuff and we went to the meeting and there were a few complaints: "Why do we have to do it?" "I work with my kid – why do I have to fill this out?" Basically the same feelings that I had when I got it. And there are a lot of moms that are going back to school themselves and one says, "I am in school and this is just extra." So, I raised my hand and I was like, I did not want to do it at first either. But, it allowed me to reflect on what I had done during the month to work with my child and I found that there were *more than five things* that I did. So it is a good 'atta-boy' for the parent because it really showed you what you had done during the month, and you just might do it – to make sure your child is well-rounded. It is still a pretty useful tool and for the mom that had said she was in school, I said your kid is seeing you do your homework. It is very powerful – especially if you are talking about what you are doing: "I am really tired but I have to do my homework" – or when you bring home the grades that you get and you show them to your child. That is a big difference. It's what they see. If you look at it as a reflection tool – [it fosters] joy or self-confidence. … and it

65

just gives us another little focus and supports what they are doing in school and it is another connection with the school and the parent.

Being vocal. Parent involvement is advocating for your child, advocating for other children, you know? And also supporting the school in whatever they need. Just sharing your ideas – that is your involvement right there. And whatever your level of comfort level is with that. A lot of parents are afraid to say something and then sometimes – I don't want to say afraid, but apprehensive. Because when I approached Jola's teacher last year, I went back and forth about do I need to really write this email? How is it going to come across? What is the tone? Am I being… I'm not trying to be *that* parent. I don't want her to think I'm like – that's my kid who is perfect. I don't. But then I had to come to the realization if I don't fight for her – who is? You know this is important – even if it comes out where I don't look right. This is something that I need to do. Because I think that some parents would have been apprehensive about approaching teachers or administrators when they have some concerns. And then other parents that may approach it in the confrontational way, which you know, then it is like… why does it have to be a fight?

So, we were doing two hours of homework – seriously? This is ridiculous and we went back and forth a little bit with the homework and there were other parents that had issues too because we wanted to do the homework right. To do all of this at home and then we went through a thing where she was not getting all of her points for her homework and I was like "look – if I am sitting up doing all this homework every night – she needs her points. It's homework, I'm a teacher. Nobody grades homework." Because it is homework, give her all her points. And I would look at her progress report… She went from making straight A's, and we were all very excited about that – to now she is making B's and I was like okay, but her tests were good and her classwork was good and it was this *homework* thing. I ended up talking to Carolyn who told me to write a letter – or send an email with my concerns. Because I had spoken to her teacher before.

I am not confrontational at all. I avoid confrontation. That is why it took me so long to get to actually address the homework issue because I – I did not – mind you I did not send the email until almost the end of the school year when [Jola] got her progress report and it was B's on there and I had been watching her grades and you know it took me a minute and I did not do it right away, I had to think about it. I need to look at her scores, I need to see a pattern – all that before I do anything. I am like *Law and Order*. I want to have my case set up, I don't want her teacher to think this is frivolous *at all*.

I sent the email to Carolyn, but I copied the principal. I did not copy the teacher, which I probably should have done, but they ended up sending it to her anyway. But I was like, I've been talking to you enough – you're not hearing me. So it ended up that she was being *just a little bit anal* about the homework. And [the teacher] said that they hold [their homework] up and put it away. "So if they don't have it on their desk or it does not look complete, then I take off points." So you are telling me that *my child doesn't have homework on the desk? More than once? (Her voice continues to escalate.) For real?!* She is not that kind of kid. She does not want to be embarrassed first of all. I wouldn't think. And *if she is* that is a *discipline* issue as opposed to an academic issue. But we got it all straightened out and she's changed her policy and it's much better.

So, um, I don't know. Maybe advocating is not a threat to the school but it can be seen as a threat to the teacher. Because the school is going to protect itself. So it is all going to come down to that individual [teacher] unless it gets to the school level. Now, if [the problem] is a *school* policy, that is how I approach it. *This* is your policy. This is what it says and when I went to the meeting, I made sure I was prepared. This is what you said was your homework policy, this is what you said was supposed to happen. So I came to it as a school policy, because as a teacher, you know, it is hard. It is hard and no matter what you say, it can be switched around, so I did not want to sound like I was attacking the teacher. But sometimes in order for your needs to be met, you have to go there. Because as a teacher – teachers think they know everything – I mean *really*. I am with your kid all day long and you are just with them at night. For real. I *see* this side of your child. I mean you think that your kid is perfect and because of the way that they behave at home or whatever, but she does not have her homework on her desk every time. But if the teacher is not following the policy – which they are so broad now – you know, we need to fix that. Parents have to advocate for their kids.

Now there is a difference between advocating for them and making excuses for them. Which I run into a lot *as a teacher,* which makes me not want – makes me more conscious for doing that for my own child. I will not make excuses for her. I will explain. Like, I will write a note if we did not have time to do homework because blah, blah, blah, like please excuse her. Now if she is doing something *wrong* – no. No. But as a teacher we have parents that say: "I don't think it is right that you are doing this." I'm like look, you have a demon! So, I will write. *I am keeping notes*! So you know, there is a difference between advocating for them and making excuses for them.

Yeah, when parents are [*too*] involved – when they are making excuses for their child. When they are trying to live, relive their childhood through their child. When they don't allow their kids to make any mistakes. When they don't allow their child to receive the consequences or the rewards for their actions… I want all her homework to be right but I am not *going to do it for her*. And there are times, there are – when I know telling her how to do it is the same as doing it for her. Now sometimes, I justify that as giving her a good example. (*She smiles.*) But when I notice that she is pimping me into doing her homework, it is like, you have taken it too far. You have messed your own self up because it was like, I was doing it, and she will be like, "I don't really understand" and I will be like, "oh its blah, blah, blah." Then you know: "well, what does such and such mean?" Go get your dictionary and please stop pimping me! And when parents don't let their children grow and make those mistakes and be imperfect – I think that is a bit too much.

Correct behavior.   When you sit down and think about it, parents have to ask themselves, is this correct behavior? I don't care what you see on TV or what your life is, you have to know [some behavior] is not okay! You have to – I mean some people don't – but you know you are cussing [a person] out because your mama cussed everybody out and now your kid is cussing everybody out. But notice that 90% of the world does not go around cussing everybody out. You know. You don't want anybody cussing *you* out. Because you puff up and make everybody scared to say anything to you – so nobody will say anything to you. So I think it sends a message. Just like suspending a kid from school or expelling a kid – it is going to send a message. Even though that is not what you want to do, sometimes it is what needs to be done. If it is affecting the environment that you are trying to have in your school. I think we should reach out to those parents who don't know – don't know and go home.

But I would think at a place like SSCES, although I am sure it does happen, but people who send their kids there want something better for their kids simply because they sent them there. Like, I needed a place for Jola to go because I could not get her into any of the other public schools. Like, well, I was not comfortable in the schools in my neighborhood just in terms of achievement and so I originally wanted her to go to a Catholic school but we could not afford it. But there is that extra layer at SSCES that may not be at some other schools. The extra layer is following the rules and guidelines and orders that are set in the school.

The push is more now schools can not do it on its own. We only have eight hours in the day at SSCES but at these other public schools where they add this extra 90 minutes, whenever they do that next June, it is still not enough time. We need your help – it needs to be a partnership and it is really important. But a lot of people are still in the same mindset that I sent [my child] to school there, they are responsible for teaching you your academics. I will teach you your social thing, or not, but why are they calling me about this? You [the teacher] take care if he is doing that. *You* take care. So, and the schools are like – I can't hit him – I can't *take care of him*.... I mean not that I am advocating hitting children that are not yours... I was talking to my friend and she is old school for real. I remember you used to get a whooping from your teacher and you would get a whooping from your mama and you better not say anything to anybody. Corporal punishment is not the best thing to do anyway, so you know as we move away from that mindset, you need more tools and the parents are the tools because they can have more consequences at home to back up what we [as teachers] are trying to do.

And getting, like you said, getting a spanking you know, that is only going to work for a minute. So, do you want punishment or do you want a whipping? Oh, I'll take a whipping. No, you don't get a choice – you are going to get them all – all the above. And they will be like – okay I won't lie anymore or whatever. And don't go to school acting like that. And don't set me up with your teacher. Do not. Because I will tell a kid in a minute: You are setting your mama up – you are setting her up.

Because when she comes in here, I am going to tell her this, this and this, and what are you going to say? And she is going to be upset because she did not get the full story from you. Don't set her up. And they are like "ok" (*imitating the child*). Do you really want *me* to call her? Because I have my list. I can go waaay back. You did not just start this. Don't set your mom up.

Perceptions and stereotypes. Yes, I am battling perceptions. Because I had those perceptions before I became a parent, since I am a teacher. I could tell a mom based on the kid's appearance. That is why I have to slick down Jola's hair because (*we both laugh*) because if a kid comes to school with their hair looking wild, [I'm thinking] what is your mama…?? Until I realized it is not that easy to get everybody up and dressed and get their hair combed in the morning. You know, it does not matter how many degrees you have or don't have – I mean, I respect the moms that have the time to get the hair done and it has the little braids in there and they look cute every morning. (*She says this as she playfully demonstrates braiding in the air.*) Now I don't know. I can assume she does not have anything else to do. *But* she might have a *whole lot of stuff* to do and that might just be her talent – that I don't have. So I had those perceptions of [Black] moms. I have only taught Black children – which comes from my good private school education – to pass my good private school education on to others who didn't have the opportunities I had. But you know, I [made judgments].
Yes, there is an overcompensation [on my part]. I need to make sure her homework is done and in order and correct. She might not be a rocket scientist, but I want the best education that I can get for her. So um, I'm lucky in a sense that I am a teacher and her teachers know I am a teacher and then that perception has additional responsibility. Because [it] could be: "here comes Jola's mom again – she thinks she knows everything cause she is a teacher and she is going to question me and she is going to make suggestions and she is going to try to rule my classroom." But I am the first to step back. Like, I am not trying to run your classroom. Like, I made a suggestion to her 2nd grade teacher. They were talking about civil rights and it was a discussion of like Susan B. Anthony or somebody and I was like well, what about Ida B. Wells – you're right here.[10] But you know, she was going by the book and she's an excellent teacher but sometimes that cultural thing gets lost and… (*her voice drops*), I said, I'll just leave her alone. I will just teach her Ida B. Wells at home. And the teacher did a really good thing and was like, "well if you want to come in and do a little piece on that or send me some stuff," and I never got a chance to send her anything and so I was like, yeah I will keep my mouth shut. But um, yeah, as just a regular Black woman without being a teacher and that other stuff, there are perceptions that I am going to be confrontational and stuff like that and I am going to baby my kid. But also with the added education that I have and the experience that I have, there can also be the perception that I am going to be overbearing, which I do not want to be. Perceptions of Black mothers – there is always going to be

that perspective – especially in Chicago. Especially in neighborhood schools a lot of times. It is going to be negative before it is positive. A lot of times. And it also depends on how you come to the teacher though.

And how you come to the school. We can look at kids that are well kept and a lot of it is reflected in your child. The care that a mother takes, and not just in education, but the care that a mother takes for her child, the way your kid goes out, is a direct reflection of you. So if her hair is standing out…. the kids hair is looking all crazy and the mother's hair is all whipped. She got the weave here and back and the kids come to school dirty. Your child is a reflection of you in education or anywhere else.

When I started teaching, that was the first time I encountered parents who were not necessarily involved or they listened to what their kids told them and not the adult. They came ready to whoop *your* tail because you were *picking on them* and you called and said that you needed to conference with them because their kid was acting up. And so you know, I learned from that. And the parent involvement – there was no parent involvement. The assemblies we had were during the day and the parents did not come. There were no "family nights" or anything like that. Parents did not have to walk their kids to school; the kids came straight out the projects down the stairs. You might see parents when somebody called but basically, *only* when you called. Now, at [another school] we had more parent involvement – not a lot more – but of course graduations and stuff, report card pick up, open house. We have more parents and there was more outreach at getting parents, and I am not sure if that has just changed or if it was just again, because of the parents in the area. Because there seems to be a lot of outreach to parents. We will call you, we will text you if there is a problem, you will have my cell number, your kid can call me up until 9 o'clock. That's two-way involvement.

SONIA[11]

Sonia held a leadership position with the parent organization. I seem to remember everyone having a pretty equal hand in responsibilities, but any loose ends were tied by her. Also, if there were concerns that the parents wanted to collectively address to the school administration beyond Carolyn or Nikki, it appeared that Sonia took the charge. Her primary responsibility was to serve as a liaison, between voicing the parents' needs and the schools' needs (including principal and teachers), so that everyone was 'on the same page.' Sonia was very vocal about her frustration and urgency to communicate more effectively as a whole, rather than on a parent-by-parent basis.

Having been introduced as a researcher in our first meeting, Sonia blatantly said to me, "I want to read what you're reading." Sonia, more than anyone, acknowledged my position as an outsider with leverage and access to information that could instigate major change. In this way, she immediately made me feel like an ally; I also felt like I had to be a better researcher. While I wanted to be comfortable as an observer, Sonia made me realize I had to 'pay off.' In many ways, Sonia made me feel like a spy. In smaller planning meetings, she would 'off the record' ask, "Well, what have you heard?" I constantly had to negotiate my position not just as researcher but a contracted employee of this school and my funders, while still making sure to prioritize the parents' needs rather than shadow them under the needs of the so-called major stakeholders. I can't say that I always dodged this bullet well, and Sonia surely held me accountable.

In the middle of the school year, Sonia relocated to another state. This had a major impact on the parents' organization as well as her personally. However, this became an incredible transition period for her. Not only had her first son – Sundiata – began college away from home, but she also remarried, and moved to an entirely different climate. She is now raising her younger son – Selassie – in a blended family with a 13, 12 and 5-year old. Due to distance, both interviews took place over the phone and lasted a total of approximately two hours.

Involved mother.   Until third grade I actually went to a school in a poorer community, quote unquote – it was in the projects. And then third through entire high school... we moved out South. Out of the projects, it was supposed to be considered a better – a higher economic situation. My mom was not active [in school]. She went on the first day and showed up for the report cards. So the irony is, my mom has her degree in child psychology and she is a teacher and all that so, it is kind of, very ironic now that I just thought about that. It was just expected, you didn't need [involvement]. You were smart, you didn't need it. Do your homework and then you can do whatever you need to do. There was no penalty or repercussion; I was valedictorian, I was head of the class, blah, blah, blah. So at home there was no support or instruction or structure, I guess. There was an *independent* structure – I will say it that way. With my mom's education if [participation] would have been more expected of her and blatant I am almost confident that she would have participated.

School choices.   Sundiata went to the same grammar school that I graduated from because I actually bought my mom's house and moved in there. And I remember getting the letters from *No Child Left Behind* saying that the school was failing. So we applied for SES's[12] program for 7th and 8th grade and he went to SES from 7th to 12th grade. For Selassie, I *knew* that the local school was not an option. I had gone to CPS fairs. Yeah, I was being more proactive because the local school was not an option. Because I knew that the schools were failing. CPS as a whole was failing, in my mind. So after I pulled Sundiata out and he went through a much different program and was much more successful, so, it just, CPS was just not an option.

My goal is to make sure that [Selassie] continues to be challenged. [Previously] my mom home schooled him. He was getting a really good education with my mom. I was still afraid that he was going to be used to having all the attention and all of that stuff, so I wanted him to be around other kids before he started kindergarten. So I had been listening and trying to learn about this whole charter school movement

71

and we applied for a few charter schools and we got into SSCES. We got into another one actually that was literally walking distance from my house at that time but I decided that SSCES with the longer school day and things like that won me over. [SSCES] really expected the children to succeed. I don't know if it was propaganda or what. Not settling and expecting the best and it seemed like they had this whole new generation of young motivated teachers and their life's purpose was to educate in the school and to the children and all of that. I would say they were consistent 110 percent. But, I don't know, the fact that there seemed to be a war between CPS and the charter schools made me feel like that the charter schools were being alienated. It was politics and the children were really not the focus and the results and other possibilities were just was not enforced.

School relationships. I actually took on [a leadership role] because the staff and culture, they were doing such a good job. Their approach to education and they way they worked with my child – that I had never seen happen. I felt like if we could get the parents involved, this would be heaven. The principal used an example of a three-legged stool and she was like we cannot achieve greatness without all three legs and the three legs are the students, the teachers, and *the parents*. It will not work if one piece is missing. And that really struck a chord with me that I know – that is how it is supposed to work. I've never seen it but I know it and believe it and I wanted to help bring that other leg – you know? Because they were doing wonders without us. If we had more participation in helping out and bringing resources and helping our children or whatever, then it would just be over the top.

I read this book um, *Outliers* by Malcolm Gladwell and I learned a new term called – cultivated parenting? (*She mumbles through a lot of words and phrases and I begin to flip through my notes really fast because I am thinking I'd just heard of the same thing. I ask, concerted cultivation?*) Concerted cultivation! (*We both laugh and sigh.*) So I may not have to break it down as much because I think you know what I'm talking about! In school there is currently no concerted cultivation – it is more of an independent, fend for yourself, figure out what you like, support you from afar – if I support you at all, kind of environment. So it seems like it would take two or three generations to get to, concerted cultivation.

I think, well, from what I have learned this year is that everybody is at a different stage and a different level. I think the intention – I think the parents have the best intentions to help and may not execute it in the best way and there might be some results – negative results from that. That is even more of a reason that the administration has to have a qualified leadership role. It can't be – it can't, I don't even think it should be – it can't be entry level as far as the qualifications for the person that is going to work with these people. How is that supposed to work? It has to be a leader – a person that is really flexible. I don't know really what the essential requirements are, but I don't even think it can be a mid-level person. I think it needs to be a higher-level person. So I don't think that people volunteer with malicious intent, because everybody is different and comes from different backgrounds and communicates differently and all of those kinds of things are normal things that make people different. But it can have some bad results if it is not handled right. We are just different. So many different backgrounds. It should definitely be the parents that identify what unacceptable behavior is, but I don't know who should correct it or adjust that. I think the parents can address it on the peer-to-peer level like, "girl, what's up? You probably don't want to do that," and that would be a really good benefit of having a parent group. But when it is something that is beyond a person's qualifications – the parent group can't be held accountable. I think the best thing for the parent group to do is get some professionals up in here and we address passive aggressively what negative parent behavior is.

Perceptions and stereotypes.   I honestly feel like there are more stereotypes against teachers – especially White teachers, but that's mostly all that comes into the Black community. I think that the stereotype that most Black mothers have, or a lot of Black mothers have against White teachers and White people is, "the White liberals are coming to save our kids" does more harm than good. I think a lot of people – a lot of parents – the stereotype that we have about "White people coming into our community help save our kids" – it causes us to be more distant from them and also makes us just get bag off and let them do *it* and that is more harmful than good. I think a lot of our behavior is based on the fact that, *that* is the stereotype.

At [SSCES], I was working against the fact that there was no expectations for us. That um, we (*referring generally to the school administrative body*) are going to make our goals and we are going to do our numbers regardless of the parent participation. That's great, that's good. But at the same time when you have some parents that have stepped up and said what do we do – we should be putting some kind of system in place to make that happen. I think some labels of Black mothers are: angry… working all day and not able to spend a lot of time with their children. Loving but maybe not as nurturing. [But] I don't feel like I have to work against these labels. My focus is more on Selassie's development and his journey versus how my approach is being judged. I don't consider that, I don't take it personally. My focus is on *him*.

Becoming mother.   I don't think I had that deep down I've ever been in a position in my life where I was like "I want to be a mother!" With Selassie, I was married and my husband didn't have any children so I was – that was a conscious decision. And honestly at that time, I felt that was my duty – as his wife – seeing that he didn't have any children. I was only 17 [when I had Sundiata]. It wasn't a decision. I was young and dumb as far as really making a conscious decision, like, "oh, I want to be a mother." The community was awesome. My mother was very vital to my success. Even my division teachers, my father, my baby daddy (*she says with a smirk*) – as much as he *could* be as a 19-year boy – his family. It was a lot of support there. And so I probably have a twisted theory on this: that much support sends the wrong message. I can see why a lot of other young, teenaged people can have, can continue to do that – can make that same mistake again with so much support and *positive feedback* about the situation. But I'm glad I had it. Sometimes in our community though that sends the wrong message.

I think there needs to be more education on why… why. The symbolism. What it means to have children. Being a mother. How that affects society. You know, affects your life. Instead of, "oh, everybody and everybody had a baby when they were 17." So there's no difference and just a bunch of babies. But can we stop this and not encourage this. But you know, it's such a fine line between having a baby and having a baby when you're of age. (*She is taking long pauses as she prepares to make this statement and stutters through several word choices.*) I don't want to say that having a baby is a curse. But at some point, families need to have those conversations. Mother means personal development. Character development. Nutritionist. Protector. Educators. Character development.

A big part of my role too, as a mother is helping my husband – be more participatory. For example, when we're talking at the table and it's Halloween and the 13-year old says, "I wanna be Nikki Minaj for Halloween." (*She shrieks and screams loudly so that we both start laughing.*) Uuum, why. Why why why? But my husband was like, "oh okay." Hmmm. So I'm like, let's look at it like this. Let's look at it like you were dating again and a woman says, "oh I wanna be Nikki Minaj…" (*Her voice raises*) You're probably not going to date her – anymore. Because that's just a different value system. So when we're at the dinner table and your daughter says she wants to be Nikki Minaj, you need to delve into that a little further and have some conversations with her about that. I can't do that [with her] yet. I do as much as I can. So another part of being a mother is being a psychologist – asking the questions like, "well okay, but *why?*" And knowing how to approach [situations like this] without shutting it down because the minute you shut it down they want to do it more. So to ask more. To evaluate more. And a lot of those conversations take place. But um, we're still trying to figure it out. And it does cause conflict because in other spaces, they do have access to things like that. Just not here. We "them bougie Negroes."

Blended family. Having a blended family looks like a lot of family meetings. A lot of discussions and respecting each other's differences. Because we even have our youngest daughter who is Muslim. So, I mean, there's so many differences with everything and everybody – socially, religiously, as far as diet is concerned. So we're always watching movies that try to, that encourage everybody's beliefs and make us open. A lot of family movies that have values about respect, being confident in yourself, learning how to make a decision, educational and value-based movies to try to balance stuff out. Because anything else is going to teach the violence or teach them confusion or teach them non-acceptance or that ridiculing people is okay. We have to be *very* careful with what we watch, what we do, what we let them have access to. To encourage difference in the family, but to also let everyone know who *they* are, and their background, is okay too.

I get a lot of pushback. I do get a lot of resistance. I'm "Nappy Swagger" and I'm in the South. I'm so opposite in so many ways, that I think, it's healthy. That eventually, maybe in four or five years, [the 13-year old] will [have casual communication] with me. We're still in the South and you know – you just don't disrespect adults. So there's that piece; there is still respect there. But I'm glad to be that different. I'm glad to be that *contrast*. It's hard. I just still stand on what I believe in and I voice my opinion. I still dictate what happens in this house – where we're gonna go, what we're gonna watch, what they're exposed to. When we go out it's very strategic. And there've been moments where I can see [the 13-year old] appreciating it. Whether or not she's willing to admit it verbally. And her dad too. He knows that what we're doing is so much better. He's very supportive. It's just a matter of pushing through and being patient. Pushing through, but not pushing anything *on* them. It's either this way or no way. (*She laughs.*) It's not like I'm *making* you do it – but *I am*. It's real passive aggressive. (*We both laugh.*)

"Mother to son." I'm exposing Selassie to a different culture, to a different education system. I do feel like I am taking risks, but I am taking calculated risks, to make him successful in this world. Only thing I worry about is the reactions that he gets from my family. You know how hard it is in the Black community, where, "yall think yall better than us." Selassie is like, "I'm not drinking *that* – I'm not drinking cow's milk." And you know you can't say that to everybody. (*We both laugh.*) And he's so danggone *smart*: "do you see any other mammals drinking other mammals' milk?! Do cows drink monkey milk?" And I'm like Selassie! You have to learn the delivery. Like, just say you prefer soy milk. So examples like this. I know this is better for his health in the long run, and he may get pushback in school, you know. The risk is in being rejected socially. That's what it is. Not being the average Black boy. And it's messed up that – that even has a label.

My mom laid it out for me, but I probably put it on steroids – I'm the next generation so I'm pushing the envelope even *more*. She taught me before I ever read a book to empower our young males – our Black males. To make them realize that they are Kings and they don't have to fall for the stereotypes and what they see on the TV or in the media. They should want to change that. And let them be okay... be okay if they're not considered cool – to go against the grain. So the best way I can protect Selassie is to prepare him. A couple of years ago, protection was more like nurturing his emotional needs – and it still is – but he's 9 about to be 10 (*she smiles as she says this*), so I have to bag off of, I want to say *babying him* (*she laughs*), however that translates – give him more independence so that as he gets older, he can really protect himself.

THE PRESENT OF PRESENCE: SUMMATION

After conducting the first interview, I had to fully understand what it meant to be the primary instrument of inquiry (Merriam, 1991). Maya was the first to agree to the interviews and I was eager to receive every word. I sat across from her in a comfortable living room chair and after opening my interview protocol in a Word document on my laptop, the GarageBand Apple application to record the audio, and setting up a separate handheld MP3 recorder, I simply decided to sit cross-legged on the floor with all the technology spread around me. I was poised to capture all the tangible and intangible moments as every textbook noted a good qualitative researcher should do. However, I fumbled for quite a bit because it all felt too awkward; Maya had invited me into an intimate space and I was slightly embarrassed for all the "wires." So I pushed the smaller recording device to the side along with my laptop – out of our immediate view. GarageBand was still running, but it wasn't situated between us and I only glanced over to look at the conversation prompts. After what seemed like forever (which was likely less than 10 minutes,) I was ready to listen.

I was so excited when I left that I almost begin scribbling my field notes in the car outside of her house; however, I sped home and again spread the technology out in front of me (after I called her to report that I'd made it home safely, which she insisted that I do). I opened GarageBand, only to find it had not recorded one word. I'd used GarageBand dozens of times but in my nervousness, I had not applied the correct settings. I immediately turned to my smaller device: Nothing. I was distraught. I began scribbling feverishly; I recall better when I use actual pen and paper. I was halfway through the first sheet of paper when the panic paralyzed me. Only one thought kindled: Call Renée. Renée is an artist, performer, writer, and critical ethnographer; she lives and breathes this work and her name was the first to pierce my brain. She answered the phone and I spilled everything I'd been thinking since the technology failed me and she calmly replied, "it's okay." I blurted, "but it was such a great conversation, she said *everything* and I got nothing!" Renée, in the most peaceful – always peaceful – voice possible asked/stated, "but you were there, right?" Of course I was there! "Well, take a deep breath and write everything you remember right now. You were there. And that's enough. Trust what you heard. Trust how you received it. Never believe a recorder is more present than your body. You didn't lose anything. You were there." And so I was. Beyond the recording and writing devices I used in subsequent interviews, the dialogue shared between myself and the mothers resonate with me every day.

The complexities of these women's narratives make it difficult to do them justice. We have clocked uncounted hours in planning meetings, social events, work lunches, Facebook conversations and of course these interviews – which have been processed and crafted from over 150 pages with approximately 62,000 words, absent of unrecorded gestures, long memory pauses, and children/partners/friends coming in and out. However, in my role as researcher, I attempted to capture the most salient themes, leaving room for tension and contradiction so that we – as an audience – may better understand not only these collective experiences but also what is being taught.

What is presented in the following chapter: "Defining Mother," "Preparing Children," "Navigating Institutions" and "Other" is a cross-sectional platform for roughly four generations of lived experiences. The subthemes such as *school choices, leadership, deconstructing Blackness* and *blended family* which are presented in this chapter warrant even more space; however, they were tangential conversations that generally chaffed an old wound of family history or the fresh wound of still *learning* mother. They are incredible markers for future conversations.

NOTES

[1] Evanston, a suburban city north of Chicago that developed around Northwestern University, is approximately 20 miles from the area in which Maya grew up. During the time she speaks of, Evanston had a growing community of middle-class African Americans.

[2] The Miss Black America pageant was created and produced by J. Morris Anderson in 1968 as a protest to the Miss America Pageant (1921). Helen Jean Ford – who represented Hattiesburg, Mississippi – was the ceremony's 8th woman to win the title crown.

[3] Chicago Transit Authority is the city's public bus system, at times regarded as an unsafe space depending on the route. In May 2009, 16-year old Blair Holt was fatally wounded on the bus traveling home from school while trying to protect a female classmate.

[4] Nikki is the only biracial mother in this project. This was brought to my attention when I asked her about what lessons she learned from her mother – assuming she was Black. This opened an intense conversation about the duality of identity that was different from the other participants. However, all of the women in this project self-identify as Black mothers.

[5] "Mother to Son" is a poem written/published by Langston Hughes (1902–1967) in 1922, which in 20 lines illuminates the struggles of motherhood and perseverance – most poignantly noted in its opening: "life for me ain't been no crystal stair…"

[6] On February 26, 2012, 17-year old Trayvon Martin was murdered while walking on a residential sidewalk in Sanford, Florida by a neighborhood watchman – 28-year old George Zimmerman – of the gated community where the boy was visiting family. According to a 911 recording, Zimmerman phoned local authorities to report a guy "who looks like he's up to no good or on drugs or something." The authorities told Zimmerman to *not* pursue; however, he continued to follow stating "these assholes always get away" and whispered the racial epithet, "fucking coons." He stepped out of his vehicle and subsequently fatally shot Martin in the chest – as he was only holding a bag of candy and a canned tea he'd just bought from the local convenient store. One month later, Zimmerman had still not been charged nor arrested and during an unrelated press conference, President Barack Obama addressed the tragedy stating: "If I had a son, he'd look like Trayvon."

[7] In the opening chapter of *The Souls of Black Folk* (1903), W.E.B. DuBois, proponent of the double consciousness theory, writes of himself between two worlds: one Black, one White. Upon interaction with those of the other world, he restates an implicit question posed to him. "Instead of saying directly, How does it feel to be a problem? They say, I know an excellent colored man in my town." DuBois continues to discuss the implications and tensions of self-determination within a dominant society of those who already claim to *know* him.

[8] The first principal of the school was responsible for opening my position. Immediately after, she was offered a promotion within the company and was transitioning and training the new principal the summer I was there to develop the University.

[9] Parent Teacher Associations and Parent Teacher Community Organizations.

[10] Ida B. Wells-Barnett (1862–1931), sociologist, journalist, suffragist, anti-lynching activist, and namesake of the low-rise development built in 1941 exclusively for Black families on the South Side of Chicago.

[11] During my second conversation with Sonia, I shared with her the pseudonym I selected for her and she responded: "ohhh! I'ma look her up on Google as soon as I get off of the phone! I'm frantic!"

[12] General pseudonym for the Selective Enrollment School where she enrolled Selassie.

CHAPTER 5

COMING TOGETHER

Analysis and Interpretations

Four themes function as an interpretative analysis of both the dominant and complementary narratives presented in Chapter 4. Three of the themes' titles are noted by action and stakeholder: "Defining Mother," "Preparing Children," "Navigating Institutions." The last theme, "Other," is titled differently because it examines the narrative of "Deja." She is the imagined other that falls out of the range of 'acceptable behaviors' previously discussed.

DEFINING MOTHER

Each mother talks about her life roles in various ways – teacher, nutritionist, protector, psychologist, nurturer. However, what is most salient is that they all position themselves as *advocates*. Whether because they were born into privilege, gained it through Catholic and private institutions, or through the close hand of their mothers, these women discuss the importance of giving back and giving more. In this way, the idea of *strength* was also repeated. It is this strength that compelled me to stay connected to these women – knowing that their stories had to be told, not as anomalies, but in a tightly threaded quilt that holds centuries of history. History and Education scholars such as James D. Anderson (1988), Joyce King & Carolyn Mitchell (1990), Vanessa Siddle Walker (1996, 2000), Heather Williams (2007), Cheryl Fields-Smith (2005), Belinda Robnett (2000), have shown us that Black mothers have a strong legacy of fighting for their children, especially when it comes to citizenship and education – often viewing them as one in the same. In this way, each mother's narrative was connected to the narrative of *her* mother and continued with the expectations for her children. These expectations are what provide the foundation for every thought and action.

Becoming a mother may not have been a conscious choice for each woman in this project – we see this range between Maya and Sonia – nevertheless, the will to push, protect, and educate their children and community is ever-present. They remind me of Assata Shakur. In the midst of several court trials, having endured 20 months of solitary confinement in the basement of a men's prison, sustaining abuse that left her nearly paralyzed and later detainment in a maximum security women's prison, Shakur made the decision to conceive a child with a long-time comrade and co-defendant who assured her: "if you become pregnant and you have a child, the child will be taken care of. Our people will not let the child grow up like a weed"

(Shakur, 1987, p. 92). In the spirit of Women Centered Networks (Hill-Collins, 2004a), Assata understood the sense of community that sustained her. While she was denied adequate medical attention that nearly aborted the child, she writes of her daughter (who is now almost 40 years old with two children of her own), "we are pregnant with freedom. We are a conspiracy" (Shakur, 1987, p. 130). Being a mother is ultimately seen as a great act of revolution.

Additionally, raising the community, or taking care of other children is second nature. Othermothering was a foreign term to the mothers I talked with; however, the concept was concrete: 'I raised my sister's kids before I had my own,' or 'yes, Mrs. B raised *me* and she helped me raise my child,' or 'his mom has a crazy work shift so I just let him stay here with my son and I take them both to school.' There are many mothers whose names are unknown to us first, because of the everyday need to push forward rather than be acknowledged and second, because their names were deliberately and painfully omitted.[1] The women of this project, who engage the taken-for-granted work of revolution right in their homes, claim both their name and their work as a continuing legacy.

Inherent to Black mother's identities is balancing the "strong Black mother image." The sanctification of Black mothers is a double-edged sword that wields an expected life of sacrifice for Black mothers as a tireless vessel for the Black community (Christian, 1985; Hill-Collins, 1990/2009; Staples, 1970/1981). In Alice Walkers' landmark essay, "In Search of Our Mother's Garden," the writer/poet asks rhetorical questions: When do our mother's rest? What art is sacrificed so that we may *live*? Where – aside from the hopes of her children – does the Black mother flourish? Acts of self-sacrifice are engrained in these narratives as Nikki stated, "girl, prepare for guilt to rule your life!" shaping the idea that whatever you do never feels like enough. Maya said plainly, it is not about you anymore and regardless of whether each mother felt that she was doing her best, I received the message that they were giving 'all they've got.' This was especially obvious to me as each mother either apologized for "talking my head" off or "taking me into too many different directions" when the truth was, anywhere they went was exactly where we needed to be. At the end of my conversation with Sonia she said, "Thank you for giving me this opportunity to reflect on things for myself. We are just on autopilot so we don't stop to reflect and know."

As demonstrated throughout this work, motherhood for Black women has never been simply and neatly bound to domestic responsibilities of home keeping and social mobility. Her role has been to assert the worth of her child/ren while fighting for both their survival and development. Her dreams like most mothers are that her children will surpass her respective status, but beyond that, many of us hope that our children will create cracks in the ceilings of oppression and ultimately break through to taste and savor the right-to-life that was not guaranteed to our ancestors and elders. Our children are born and shaped with the weight of salvation – whether it is an individual actualization or reaching the highest hope of salvation for an entire community. And this is what makes Black motherhood revolutionary: we hope for our children the privilege of absolute freedom and no fear.

Defining Mother teaches us that there are several different entry points for motherhood but a renewed sense of purpose drives each woman forward, engendered by self-reflection. This includes a connection to a historical legacy of advocating for our children while also checking the pulse of contemporary concerns; creating strategies for how we expose our children; accepting the obligation of leveraging privilege to take care of our community; and submitting to the idea of strength and self-sacrifice for the fulfillment of what we believe is greater than us.

PREPARING CHILDREN

When the mothers talked specifically about parent involvement, it was most often in the context of the school. Whereas this appears to be the traditional way we conceptualize parent involvement as a schooling process, this is not in fact how the mothers' families functioned. Relating the stories of how their own mothers were involved, the responses were, 'they showed up for report cards', or they weren't involved at all. In fact, when the SSCES parents were preparing to organize 'involvement meetings,' Sonia said she was looking for "anything I could find on Google to help!" However, their involvement is better highlighted when the mothers talk about how they engage and prepare their children for the world outside of their homes. Sonia briefly touched on this in our conversation when she brought up the idea of concerted cultivation. Educator and sociologist Annette Lareau explores this process in her work, *Unequal Childhoods* (2003). We see this in full play as we are brought into the discussions between the mothers and their children as well as the "organized activities" that they have "established and controlled... By making certain their children have these and other experiences, middle-class parents engage in a process of concerted cultivation" (pp. 1–2). These women talk about involvement in ways that are not always charted in expensive curricula or statistical spreadsheets, but in specific ways that build an awareness of race, character development, leadership, and responsibility into daily activities.

While economic class is not a subject that was met head-on in every conversation, there were several references to moving away from home neighborhoods that weren't safe or productive, into areas that had more affluence and promise. One of the exceptions is Nikki, who emphasizes that she grew up in the suburbs and didn't ride the CTA. However, she chose to move herself and Nkrumah into Hyde Park – a multi-cultural neighborhood that hosts an Ivy League university; a mix of 'mom and pop shops,' small Black businesses, and food co-ops; the Chicago coastline and of course, The Obamas. She says it had been her dream to grow up there because, "God, I would be so much more comfortable in my skin had I been in an environment that was more *accepting* of my skin." This urge for acceptance is the product of a long-fermented generational wound. Nikki described her father as a fair-skinned Creole man from New Orleans: "His father had fair skin and passed for White. One day my father was sent to his job on an errand for his mother. A coworker of my grandfather announced that 'some nigga kid is here to see you.' My grandfather came to the front of the store only to say, 'I don't know that kid' and walked away." The denial of his father subsequently rendered race – more specifically Blackness – a 'quiet' subject in her house. However, after being exposed to university courses that gave her historical context for her life experiences, she claimed a name for her child that he would not be able to turn away from. Promise for many of these women translates into personal acceptance and autonomy.

Preparing their sons and daughters as Black children is the most salient of all subjects covered in our conversations. It is talked about directly, in assumed ways, and also in contradictory terms. For example, Maya insists that she not will not raise Mursi as Black or White but as a person in a multicultural world. She was raised with experiences that allowed her to value meritocracy. She emphasizes spirituality, education, and work ethic asserting, "there is money out here to be made; how are you going to position yourself to get it?" At the same time, she lives in a neighborhood where they have to cross police lines to enter their front door. When she talks about her childhood, she is animatedly pointing in either direction to indicate 'that is the block I played with friends,' 'that is the block where so-and-so lived,' 'that is the block where so-and-so worked.' She states, "this is a building full of [us]" and lists every family member that lives on each floor. She is proud to tell me the same woman that raised her, also had a hand in raising Mursi. She has made the decision to remain in this area for the value of kinship and community. While this may not be widely regarded as expressly Black, I understand this as part of an effort to maintain Women Centered Networks and the value of Othermothering (Hill-Collins, 2004a).

Nikki talks about how she worried too much in naming her son but was acutely aware of the challenges he would face because of his skin color. Bestowing upon him a name that is so identifiably "Black" she not only demands that he acknowledge his difference but provides the opportunity to embrace it. At the same time, Sonia struggles with raising her son to *not* be the "average Black boy." She notes that while eating in a restaurant on 79th street, she is anxious about anything her child may say to have him stand out or be embarrassed but she made the "calculated risk" to raise him "differently." Sonia, Nikki, and Maya explicitly discuss raising their children to preserve who they are in a world that may choose to reject them while making space for how they will construct and claim their own identities. Each child is taught his/her *difference*, and I make the argument that none of these children are raised to see Black as a deficit.

These women teach survival. When they share their discussions of STDs, Khadafi, Sandusky or stories of letting a 12-year old ride the bus alone (something my mother and father were too afraid to let me do until I was well into high school), I am reminded of Mamie Till Mobley's choice. She revealed her child's bloated, tortured face to the world to peel back the naivety of race relations in this country and open honest conversations within our families, our government, and our world. The truth is "gut-wrenching" at times, but these mothers take the risk to be boldly honest.

As Maya points out, we may be raising children in the 21st century, but "old school" still works. This is framed with ideas such as "I am your mother, not your friend," and "nobody can take your education away from you" and opens conversations for how these mothers build character and leadership into daily activities through respect and reciprocity. These lessons are evidenced most in how they talk about their children's schooling experiences; this is where the mothers can see their work in action – how their children interact with those in their immediate world. Maya uses buying expensive designer homework binders as a lesson to show Mursi that she needs to be different from the popular girls in her classroom: "You have to start thinking like an 8th grader if you want to get through the 7th grade." Nikki notes the behavior change in Nkrumah when she separated from her partner of 10 years. In each instance, she coached her son through understanding his decisions and reminding him that she is raising him to "fight for the weaker person." Additionally, Nikki did not have these conversations in isolation but included her partner to maintain the continuity of family. Jill laughs when she talks about accepting the responsibility of Jola growing up. She is honest in saying that she was so accustomed to doing things for her as a baby and toddler, that she too had to accept Jola becoming a "big girl." So as Jola became older and knew exactly how to push mommy's buttons, Jill recognized her independence and stepped back to keep her daughter from "pimping her." These conversations – especially where Nikki reminds Nkrumah of "white boy language" and sexual safety or when Sonia discusses raising Selassie as a king, even when he doesn't fit in – are incredibly reminiscent of the work of Joyce King and Carolyn Mitchell (1990). This work – *Black Mothers to Sons* – echoes the same concerns, risks, and obstacles. Their mother work emphasizes the tools of Black cultural mores such as mutuality, reciprocity, spirituality, deference, responsibility, and language interactions. These tools are fluid through every lived experience and every shared narrative. Whether it is understanding their budding personalities, dealing with resisting authority or falling in with what is popular, the mothers are transparent in revealing the complexities of raising their children.

Preparing Children teaches us that although "parent involvement" is a remote concept connected to in-school practices, the mothers in this project fully accept the responsibility of child development. This includes teaching survival through conversations and daily interactions that bear no resistance to truth and carry the intergenerational messages of their families; placing value on who their children are as Black bodies in a discriminating and multicultural world; accepting that their "babies" will be adults by actively listening to them; and using everyday moments as teaching tools for independence and leadership.

NAVIGATING INSTITUTION

School is an institution that maintains a gatekeeping system including behavior and language norms, and access to greater resources; therefore, in addition to their motherwork, these women are holding the school accountable for helping ensure social mobility and to secure what no one can take away from them – their education. Every mother in this project expressed disappointment with the public school system's ability to do this. While this is not a total indictment of CPS, it is a reflection of how these women's experiences shaped the expectations for their children. They commuted from various neighborhoods across the city, by bus, train, or carpool to a place where they believed the staff was passionate about ensuring the success of their child, extended the values they teach at home and sustained relationships built on effective communication.

During my conversation with Carolyn, she provided an example for when effective communication was challenged. It initially involved Khoi and a male classmate. She regarded the incident as not much more than a case of unnecessary teasing that could be easily amended by either parent; however, in this case, the other child's parent was a faculty member as well. Obviously Carolyn had a relationship with both the child and the parent and felt comfortable enough to engage the child in a discussion of his relationship with her daughter. The mother of the boy responded with immense anger and reminded her of the school's rule that *parents* are not allowed to engage with other children. While Carolyn admits she was fully aware of this policy and notes that it has been effective in some cases, she thought their specific relationship opened additional ways of communication but was incredibly disappointed at how wrong she was. Carolyn saw herself as an othermother, concerned for both her own child and her classmate while she was viewed as a meddlesome parent whose concerns needed to be mediated by the school.

Shortly after the SSCES Parent University and Beacons did not reach their full potential to bridge sustainable relationships across the school, the administration began to implement, *I Care*. Every mother discussed an initial resistance to the program. Some expressed frustration that not only was it something else to do in an already tight schedule, but it was attached to their children's homework. Carolyn explained that this very expensive program was purchased to foster greater relationships in the school. As Jill noted, the teachers can not meet the expectations of successful child development by themselves, which is strikingly different from how all the mothers discussed the teacher practices of their formative schooling experiences. The SSCES Board recognized the importance of parent involvement, just as Jill was clear that she did not want to be told what to do with her child. After the initial meeting where the parents were able to express how they incorporated the requirements of the program into their day, they became more receptive, even referring to it as "excellent." Jill later says that it can serve as an "atta boy" for parents who haven't acknowledged all of the little things they do for their children. However, converting these experiences into data, coupled with the high turnover rates of both teachers and students at SSCES, certainly makes this curriculum worth exploring in great detail. For the scope of this work, I can only account for the mothers' one-month experience with the program. It appeared that it many ways, despite the ways the mothers have observed the 'puppet strings,' the implementation of *I Care* curriculum reflected the same sentiments of previous parent involvement frameworks discussed in Chapter 2. Two things worth noting here: 1. The mothers interviewed for this project have served in various leadership roles in the school and are likely more receptive to understanding the benefit of administrative decisions. 2. Maya did not talk at all about the program.

While Sonia jokingly commented that her mother laid out a plan and because she is the next generation, she put it on steroids, this is evidenced most in Maya's efforts to enroll Mursi into two highly selective enrollment schools in the city. The first school not only requires testing but has a lottery system as well. A year before Mursi was qualified to enroll, Maya assembled a portfolio of all Mursi's school records, several recommendations from her schools' administrative faculty, teachers, community sponsors, and documentation of her extracurricular activities. After several attempts, she secured a meeting with the principal of one of her prospective middle schools. Of course the principal does not vote on or enroll a specific child, but Maya simply wanted to make sure that she knew her daughter by name and credentials: "yes sir! Gave her a nice little folder with her name on it." This behavior is antithetical to the belief that Black mothers do not care about their children's education as well as the argument that Black mothers do not know how to negotiate within this institution. True, it takes a certain amount of access, research, self- awareness, and training to operate the way that Maya does, but, she is not an anomaly; her behavior simply has favorable outcomes that are collapsed into successful middle-class models.

Navigating Institution teaches us that although every mother has a different handle on access and resources, there are common goals that need to be addressed. This includes the facilitation of effective communication and mutual respect; pushing past what is expected (or not expected) of us as Black mothers and creating a greater expectation for our children; and conferring our privilege to make doors out of walls.

OTHER

Understanding the relationship between mother and teacher as co-parents requires the communication of common goals. As the school environment represents several different things to these women, modes of communication can function differently. For some, this is a place where you defer to another person's expertise, for some it is a place of work, and for others it is a service you are entitled to in providing care for your children. Each perspective of this place will determine how behavior shifts (or not). For example, Jill is very direct in dealing with her daughter yet because she is a teacher and self-described as non-confrontational, it will take her a quarter of a year to draft an email to her child's teacher regarding a homework concern because she has taken the time to examine every avenue and consequence in her mind before she speaks and acts. Nikki, who resents being identified as "soft," laughs as she describes a recent incident on the train where she confronted a couple of young girls for getting in her space. She is serious when she lets me know, in no uncertain terms, that she can fight if she has to. Maya takes advantage of the required home visits, opening lines of frequent communication with Mursi's teachers by providing email, cell and work phone information. Carolyn's behavior is complicated as she is a parent and administrator within the building, so her resolve is outwardly more calm and calculated. These women's narratives speak directly to and against the mythological apathetic, unloving, lazy images that are constructed about Black mothers; concerted cultivation works in their favor to produce 'good' behavior.

If then, the institutions favor "good revisionist Mammies," (Austin, 2003, p. 305) how do we address the "Bad Black Mother (BBM)?" (Hill-Collins, 2004b). In discussing the culture of SSCES, Carolyn says:

> So when we have open enrollment our only criteria is that the kids are a resident of Chicago, so they are able to come. If we have space, you are more than welcome. And because we are located where the projects used to be, we get a lot of students and families from that area – some that are great to deal with and others that aren't. They have grown up with a certain mindset and this is how they want their lives to be and they have that sort of, I hate to use the word, but 'ghetto mentality.' They say whatever is on their mind and walk and dress inappropriately, use inappropriate language around their children.

In every conversation I had with the mothers (with the exception of one), they pointed directly at a woman who fit this description: Deja.

The examples of Deja that are provided throughout this work paint a broader picture of Black women who are publically regarded as the bitch or the BBM as "images of working-class Black women" (Hill-Collins, 2004b, p. 123). She is the same mother that challenged my perceptions during our first parent meeting. Deja was not a quiet woman: she made her professional and personal struggles known as she reached out for help. The Executive Board of the Beacons elected Deja into a leadership position because as Carolyn said, "we felt that this would be a turn around for her." With three children and three nieces/nephews in the school, she believed she had a major stake there. It was obvious that she felt a great deal of support there, largely due to Carolyn. Some of the mothers saw promoting Deja as an opportunity to fish for others who initially may not have been willing to be involved at the school. However, not everyone felt the same. I observed many times when she came into the school building during the middle of the day to volunteer and was politely ushered to the back offices where she would be less of a distraction. Deja was restless, undervalued but most of all, not a 'good fit'.

Nikki notes that during the parent meeting, it was Deja who raised the first objection to *I Care*.

The teachers were there and you know. I don't want White people to recognize this – like it is family. It's like I see it and I don't want you to talk about it. So she was just, "I don't understand... (*She raises her voice*) I mean..." I think that she actually did say that "this is stupid" – and at that point she was behind me – she always comes near me, so I turned around and I was like "shhh" and I have never done that to her but she knows me well enough that I am going to be like, "Deja – stop!" Because at that point she was talking under her breath, but loudly, so I had to like "shush" her like twice but quietly and was a little afraid but I just had to tell her like "stop, you are – there are too many parents here for you to just be shitting all over this program, if you don't want to do it, then your child is just going to suffer for it." I know being a good parent is important to her and being a good role model is important to her, and when you got that stress on your shoulders and you are trying to raise these kids, you can't think straight, you can't put your ducks in your row and stay on that path. Nobody talks about this is a woman who finished her, I think her Associate degree and she has been looking for a job. I looked at her resume and it was pretty good...

Deja left before the meeting even ended. Overall, her role as a leader in the school had backfired. It spread through the school pretty quickly that she later slapped the new principal while in her office. Even though Nikki and Carolyn have noted that they have been working with the principal on her delivery and communication with these mothers, Deja's behavior is still unacceptable. She was temporarily banned from the school, but many parents avoided The Beacons altogether because they did not want to be associated with Deja's negative attitude and confrontational behavior. Jill notes: "It's a lot of trial and error. You don't want to alienate them, you don't want to be confrontational with them, but um – you know." Other parents like Sonia said,

I tried! I did! I tried. I tried. But sometimes you need a professional to help. A lot of people had that "hey girl" conversation but she was beyond my qualifications of what I could do. And I don't think it's color, I think it's class, or social economic conditions. But unfortunately we are always the ones who have to swallow it. Surely there are other people that act the same way. They don't have the money to do what they want to do and it's not just Black moms, but maybe it's just *poor moms?*

I hear the words of Nigerian writer and activist, Chimamanda Adiche (2012): "dignity and love matter just as much as bread and water", which remind me that Deja deserves a space just as all others. Deja represents more than one woman in one school. She represents someone who deserves to have her story listened to – without judgment or a fix. While she does not have the privileges of light skin or private school, all of us that have come in contact with Deja can see her power. As Hill-Collins notes (2004b), "representations of Black women as bitches abound in contemporary popular culture and presenting Black women as bitches is designed to defeminize and demonize them." Moreover,

> among African American Studies undergraduate students at the University of Cincinnati, the consensus was that 'bitch' and 'Bitch' referenced two distinctive types of Black female representations. All women potentially can be 'bitches' with a small 'b.' This was the negative evaluation of 'bitch.' But the students also identified a positivist valuation of 'bitch' and argued (some, vociferously so) that only African American women can be 'Bitches' with a capital 'B." Bitches with a capital 'B' or in their language, 'Black Bitches,' are super-tough, super-strong women who are often celebrated. They may be right. (pp. 123–124)

She was not asked to take a leadership position by chance. She reminds me of the woman who is famous for saying "I'm sick and tired of being sick and tired." Fannie Lou "Hamer had not been taught to be ashamed of herself her body, her strong voice" (Giddings, 1984, p. 301). Moreover, I believe that within every narrative constructed here, we all see a bit of Deja in ourselves; however, we have learned when and where to shift, which often leaves her deflated, not *celebrated.*

Deja is not intimidated – she feels like she has just as much of a right to expression as anyone else. Schools argue that not enough Black mothers are involved, but when Deja comes around, she is not welcome. So *where* does she fit? How does her voice shape the culture? In what ways are we asking her to change? In what ways is she punished when she does not? I present these questions here because I have not had the opportunity to converse with Deja. We'd had several conversations regarding work and church while I was still at SSCES; however, after several attempts to reach out to her for this project, I concluded that she did not want to take part. For a woman who is so vocal, I have repeatedly questioned, why/how did this project silence her? As she rejected the norms of the school, she also subconsciously and consciously distanced herself from the other parents. Her actions suggest there were ways she felt betrayed and violated.

My role, having been seen as part of the administration, gave her cause to cut off communication with me as well, in addition to the fact that I began to assert myself as researcher – both positions making her vulnerable and subject to more harm. Still, her silence does not make her invisible; it is an active choice. Therefore, I must acknowledge how critical she is within and alongside these narratives. Deja is our Sapphire. Critical Race Feminist Regina Austin notes, "There are so many things to get riled about that keeping quiet is impossible. We really cannot function effectively without coming to terms with Sapphire. Should we renounce her, rehabilitate her, or embrace her and proclaim her our own?" (Austin, 2003, p. 301).

Deja teaches us that for all the obstacles we face and climb as Black women, for all of the pride we plant in our children, we are granted access to places that leave *Others* behind. We recognize this in our attempts to provide assistance, to facilitate conversations, to recognize her strengths; however, when our efforts to "mold" bare no fruit, we return to our safe spaces to gear up for our own battles. We can not recognize how to redeem her while still in constant negotiations to redeem ourselves; this becomes both a personal and public pain.

RETURNING TO THE JOURNAL

These narratives and themes pushed me to return to my reflexive journal. As noted in Chapter 1, journaling throughout this process was crucial to capture both the shifts in my perspectives – as well as the mothers' – and our evolving relationships. It was not my intent for this project to sound like the dream of an ethnographic researcher. There were certainly uncomfortable places and exchanges. For example, Deja is essential to this project; she is the mother that many of the others pointed to as a case study of 'what not to do.' While the priority of every mother I interacted with appeared to be what is best for their children, it was mutually agreed that Deja did not do this the 'right way.' In other words, because there is no "manual" as Maya and Nikki pointed out, there were spaces when the mothers only asserted what was right, when it was juxtaposed with what was wrong. I then spent quite a bit of energy – on my own – trying to pinpoint what *is* the right way?

I shared with these mothers the understanding that school is a vehicle for social mobility and access; however, the schooling process, especially in a high-stakes, urban environment also leaves much room for symbolic (and obviously escalating to physical) violence. I was led to questions of how we reinscribe the White middle-class norms that are critiqued earlier in this project and how/where do we draw lines about how we confront issues that concern us and our children. Who draws these lines and who is trusted to mediate? Then, where are our markers of accountability and remediation? These are questions that require more than two rounds of interviews and are ripe for further investigation in an additional project.

It can also not be ignored that the reason I was brought into the school was to create a program that had previously been delegated to another member of its staff. In this way, there were obvious issues with respect and value of school leadership that were intensified by race and class. There were many times I positioned myself as a sheep because either that is how I felt or that is how I felt I had to perform. After my time with the program ended, I realized that making the school the central point of conversation not only was too fresh of a wound to pick but it further marginalized the parents' experiences as mothers and as women.

Other points of major consideration were shifts in school leadership, family choices due to the job market, and academic performance concerns which have had major impacts on these women's lives from the time I met them in 2010 through present. These shifting locations meant that rules and practices for today would not hold for tomorrow. Additionally, relationships I initially thought were open and transparent, at times shifted into safe conversations and tight lips once the recorder started.

Why do I bring these things up? Because there were real tensions throughout this process. I do not discuss them all in detail because they are not central to what I want to address, but I identify them as the politics of this space, which was always contextual and mobile. These tensions created points of comparison, dictating the ways these mothers discussed advocacy for their children to meet the expectations of both society and the schooling institution as well as their relationships with one another. There were several smaller conversations in addition to the interviews revealing that it took time to build relationships and larger conversations. I most certainly represented an institution no matter how I fashioned myself. This is evidenced by the length and quality of time as well as the location the mothers chose to interact with me. There were times I could tell they were not comfortable with not being able to provide an answer to a question, or to finish a story, almost like I was a news reporter demanding they give me an accurate 'scoop.' It is here they created a new space to protect themselves or outwardly resolve issues that they hadn't paused to reflect upon before. During some of these times I wanted to turn the recorder off; however, I was included in these acts. I was invited to be part of the "we."

For reciprocity to occur in these spaces, all of the participants (the mothers and I) had to be honest about who and where we were. "It is through dialogue that we resist the arrogant perception that perpetuates monologic encounters, interpretations, and judgments" (Madison, 2005 p. 167; Conquergood, 1982). This included sharing a range of stories in how we sometimes doubt ourselves as women, mothers, daughters, and the practices we engage that sustain us – whether through community, spirituality, family, or the commitments to our children. This has allowed some of us to maintain relationships that move beyond SSCES and this project.

These four themes and reflections do not cover the expanse of what is and can be learned from these narratives; this is a simple glimpse that works to untangle the dominant discourses that are consumed without question. Defining, Preparing, and Navigating call for us to investigate the structures that we actively work against every day to understand and embrace the complexities and contradictions within ourselves, including the Other. As stated earlier, as much as this work is for us to affirm and reveal, it is also about creating networks and connections to advocate a better society for our children and the generations that will follow them.

In the following chapter, I do not identify it as a conclusion but rather "Openings." Corrine Glesne (1997) writes: "conclusions suggest an ending, a linear progression that can be resolved in some neat way. I see no conclusions here, but rather *openings*" (p. 218). Therefore, I transition from the mother's narrative and open further discussion for what this work means in a larger context – beyond Chicago, and what each of us can/will contribute as community change agents.

NOTE

[1]   In the landmark Oliver Brown et al. V. Board of Education of Topeka et al. decision of 1954 (Brown v. Board), the plaintiffs in the case included 12 women: Darlene Brown, Lena Carpenter,

Sadie Emmanuel, Marguerite Emerson, Shirla Fleming, Zelma Henderson, Shirley Hodison, Maude Lawton, Alma Lewis, Iona Richardson, Vivian Scales, Lucinda Todd; and one man, Oliver Brown. Mr. Brown was the primary plaintiff not because the names are listed in alphabetical order. To present the case before the Supreme Court, the National Association for the Advancement of Colored People (NAACP) insisted a man – of good standing in the community – lead the docket to provide more substance and credibility to the case, thus rendering the 12 women invisible both politically and historically.

OPENINGS

Our narratives demonstrate that the rules and definitions of law, media, and academia are permeable because there are multiple ways of knowing and *being*. This is most obvious when considering our interactions within the school institution. Both parents and teachers are trained through lived experience; however, this space often creates a friction-bearing paradigm of power relations. Schools are assumed to be filled with *children experts* while mothers are seen as *home experts*. These worlds have a delicate relationship that can only be shifted by acknowledging the power in both spheres and leveraging it for the mutual benefit of our children. This work does not propose a mandate or sanction a program that can facilitate this need. Instead, we open space within various literature for Black mothers to speak for themselves rather than be spoken for. This chapter explores broader meanings for society and one another; greatest contributions through various dialogical exchanges; and offers short prose and a poetic transcription of "we."

BROADER MEANINGS

Chicago is the third most populated city in the country, with an approximate 2.7 million residents (U.S. Census Bureau, 2010); I have chosen to share the stories of five. In *Critical Ethnography* (2005), D. Soyini Madison asks the researcher to consider "How is the specificity of the local story relevant to the broader meanings and operations of the human condition?" These women speak back to the dominant ideas, explicitly and implicitly presented to us every day. These women have demonstrated for us the fluidity of language, class, race, and wisdom while under the constant threat of surveillance and persecution – whether on a New York billboard, a scientific journal article, or current legislation.

For example, in March 2012, Senate Bill 507, which was sponsored by Republican Senator Glenn Grothman, will "require the Child Abuse and Neglect Prevention Board to emphasize that non-marital parenthood is a contributing factor to child abuse and neglect" ("Glenn Grothman," 2012). The proposed law states:

Section 1. 48.982 (2) (g) 2. of the statutes is amended to read:

48.982 (2) (g) 2. Promote statewide educational and public awareness campaigns and materials for the purpose of developing public awareness of the problems of child abuse and neglect. In promoting those campaigns and materials, the board shall emphasize *nonmarital parenthood as a contributing factor to child abuse and neglect.*

Section 2. 48.982 (2) (g) 4. of the statutes is amended to read:

> 48.982 (2) (g) 4. Disseminate information about the problems of and methods of preventing child abuse and neglect to the public and to organizations concerned with those problems. In disseminating that information, the board shall emphasize *nonmarital parenthood as a contributing factor to child abuse and neglect.*

This bill has been proposed at the same time women are not allowed to have a voice in our reproductive rights[1] or are called "slut"[2] when to we create alternate spaces to be heard. This bill is another threat of criminalization of women and families, as both women and specifically – Women of Color – lead the nation in single-parent homes by 79%. According to an analysis performed by the Population Reference Bureau (PRB) of the U.S. Census Bureau's 2009 Current Population Survey,

> nearly one-fourth (24 percent) of the 75 million children under age 18 lives in a single-mother[3] family. Of the 18.1 million children in single-mother families, 9.2 million are under 9 years of age. About one-sixth (16 percent) of White children live in single-mother families, compared with one-fourth (27 percent) of Latino children and one-half (52 percent) of African-American children. (Mather, 2010, p. 1)

SB507 takes my attention because four of the mothers in this project have identified as "single." In what part of their narratives did you hear *abuse* and *neglect*? We, the women of this project have revisited DuBois' 109-year old question "how does it feel to be a problem?" by noting the race problem is not just the problem of Black women (and men), but the whole of society.

We Can Speak for Ourselves provides a foundation for further research that creates thick descriptions of mothers who interface with systems – especially school systems – on a daily basis and must adapt to the rapid changes engendered by reform, personal expectations and everyday life. These mothers make a private space public to engage critical dialogue of literature that determines the position of Black families in the U.S. while strengthening various networks to co-create action agendas. Their stories propose work that requires researchers, practitioners, curriculum designers, and advocates to look within, across, and beyond systems to leverage networks of power by incorporating the lived experiences of these key stakeholders and understanding how their voices have implications for a major 21st century city and beyond.

Just as we are speaking *for* ourselves, it is equally critical to note that we are speaking *to* ourselves. The narratives and lives of Maya, Nikki, Carolyn, Jill, Sonia and Deja demand an honest and self-named space so that we collectively see more than Mammy, Sapphire, Tragic Mulatto, Jezebel, Crack Whore, Baby Mama, or Welfare Queen when a Black female body walks by or *shows up*. We do not claim Black women and mothers are currently invisible – quite the contrary. This project aims at our *hyper*-visibility. We do not deny our anger, pain, passiveness, sensuality, aggression, compassion – we *risk* further public scrutiny by sharing these truths with our children because these are all natural human emotions and characteristics that make up parts, not wholes. Therefore, these "parts" should not define and confine our bodies. We are making r/evolution an everyday practice (G. Gordon, personal communication, 2012), thereby expecting our dynamic individuality to be acknowledged and to be called by our names – the names birthed to us or the names we claim for ourselves. We pull one another in and out of ourselves for strength, affirmation and to help extend our reach to give and receive love.

GREATEST CONTRIBUTIONS

In addition to "broader meanings," D. Soyini Madison (2005) also asks us to consider, "how will your work make the greatest contribution to equity, freedom, and justice?" Effective communication must take place between one another if we intend to have meaningful relationships and an impact on society. In this way, justice is about (re)presentation and dialogic exchange (Freire, 1970/2000). These exchanges can take place between mother-legislator; mother-researcher; mother-mother; mother-teacher, with the understanding that dialogue must occur often, and between varied agents. The nuanced perspectives of child advocacy, complexities of our expectations, histories of our community, and alignment of our beliefs, better inform all conversations of what it means to be involved as a Black mother.

The first conversation must address Black women as whole beings – not one or the other but as a compound: blackwoman. One of the primary charges of this work is to extend these conversations beyond the familiar – to make *power* hear. We can not shy away from discussions of race and gender; the greatest inequality is treating unequal people as if they are equal (Peter, 1981). Acknowledgement of intersectionality allows us to draw on the complexities of identity then the injustices faced as an *other*. This entry point of conversation is not intended to make Black women stand on yet another stage but opens space for mutual transparency. "In part, what makes race a confounding problem and what causes many people to not know what race is, is the view that the problems of race are the problems of the racial minority. They are not" (Delgado & Stefancic, 2001, p. 42). We obviously *see* difference; therefore, we must acknowledge as much to transform our conversations of race construction and to then trace and leverage circuits of power. "Difference must be not merely tolerated, but seen as a fund of necessary polarities between which our creativity can spark like a dialectic" (Lorde, 1979/2007, p. 11). This engenders a second conversation that offers possibilities for others to see themselves in these stories. We continuously create and recreate new "angles of vision" (Hill-Collins, 2004a, p. 49), because when people can see their reflections (their humanity, their children), they are more inclined to act.

The second conversation we engage must take care for how we assign names to ourselves, our spaces, and our ideas. This is a critical contribution toward the construction of knowledge. For example, when I talked about *othermothers* to the

95

women of this study, they were generally dismissive. Not because the idea was foreign or inapplicable. To the contrary, these women have been engaging this *practice* for generations. So when I talked formally about this idea and they waved a hand, I found later in the conversations they would talk exactly to this point describing how many children they raised or were raised with throughout their lives. Naming had the potential to end the conversation before it even started. However, I persisted with such terms to create space for shared access to various discourses. This persistence addresses the point I raised by John Stanfield (1985) in the Introduction chapter, that this work we undertake is often deemed invalid. I attribute this to the problem of a narrow discourse. To name and examine subjects and spaces advances empirical evidence that is almost exclusively understood by *only* the researcher – which additionally does not highlight intellect as much as it speaks to the protection of a ruling class (West, 1982/2003). To share this privileged language potentially unlocks gates for institutional support.

Finally, if we then subscribe to the belief that language is our tool for action, then how and when in our conversations do we create new discourses? How do we co-create knowledge? What ideas are missed when they are not named? What ideas are lost in an attempt to "claim" them? The process of naming can be both a limitation and a benefit, but the means and ends must be cofacilitated by each participant. Who will listen? Who will act? Each body must define for him/herself the ideas of equity, freedom, and justice – before, during, and after they are at the proverbial table with one another; with these questions we create new projects. We are not simply teaching others who we are but extend an invitation to holistically learn who all of us are. We collectively become "invested agents in a worldwide community" ("Mecca", Alexander Craft et al., 2007).

WE

We have learned to switch our codes, our bodies, our tones – for work, the academy, our partners, our children, and sometimes even for ourselves (Alexander Craft et al., 2007). These movements are an artform – a lifelong practice that are as natural as breath and just as necessary. The successes of Black women are celebrated, but each of us has to painfully acknowledge that we function in a country that has not meant for us to survive, much less flourish (see Figure 1). We are asked to enjoy prominent visibility as the "first", "one of the few," or the "only" (Hill-Collins, 1990/2009). We are all *exceptions,* and we push our children toward the unimagined parts of our dreams. We are so busy, so hurt, so determined, so curious, so dynamic, so full…

We say "Giiirl…" in a space of comfort, and we expect one another to understand. I am grateful these women allowed this project to serve as that space. Conversely, Nikki poignantly expressed the sentiment that we don't want to hang our laundry on the line, but we do not live in vacuums. We construct and co-perform knowledge to teach ourselves, one another, and our world that we exist. In our gardens, we must create windows for light – and be aware of those who will peek in. We talk because you need to be clear that decisions should not be made without us. We talk because when you speak to our children, we want you to know where they come from – where *we* come from. And how long that journey has been (and still is). What holds true for Maya, Nikki, Carolyn, Jill, Sonia, and Deja is personal and sacred; yet they graciously share these stories because we are *all* in and out of one another's lives every day. We take our departure from the joy, sacrifices, and theories of our foremothers and assert our power to Define, Prepare, and Navigate.

We take risks every day. When we put our children on the bus. When we speak up for those who are silent. When we correct those who are loud. And every. single. one. of. us wants to be understood. We want our children to remember our sacrifices rather than our mistakes. We want our children to know that they are worth every minute of our lives.

home[4]

mother
like teacher:
think. KNOW. feel. want. need.
time.

people
see things
one way:
SCHOOL.

Black child,
just go –
make way.
lot way.

get going Black child,
just go.

NOTES

[1] On February 16, 2012, the House Oversight and Government Reform Committee convened a two-panel hearing to discuss contraceptive mandates proposed by the Obama administration. The first panel consisted entirely of men, which created an outcry for the lack of female representation on an issue that directly affects them.

[2] While little credence should ever be given to Rush Limbaugh, it is important to note his vicious, verbal attack on Georgetown University Law student Sandra Fluke (February 29, 2012) after she gave a speech at an unofficial congressional event in support of free mandated contraceptives at her school. Limbaugh berated her for nearly 10 minutes – the softest parts of his tirade were calling her a "slut" and a "prostitute."

[3]   In this PRB brief, single-mother families are defined as families headed by a female with no spouse present – living with one or more, never-married children under age 18. Single-mother families are a subset of female-headed families, which include mother-child families as well as children in the care of grandparents or other relatives. In 2009, there were 19.6 million U.S. children residing in female-headed families. Additional analyses were provided based on educational and economic status.

[4]   This poetic transcript was taken from the collected narratives of Chapter 4. It is composed only of the 25 most frequently used words, including the title.

"IF I COULD WRITE THIS IN FIRE, I WOULD WRITE THIS IN FIRE"[1]

Epilogue

If we don't love our own babies, who is gonna do it for us? Get yo' babies. I don't care what's wrong wit 'em: ugly, pretty, sweet, bad, retarded [sic], it don't matter – get yo' babies. If you don't tell 'em you love, if you don't hold 'em, if you don't make 'em feel good about [themselves], they gon' get in the streets and have hatred in they heart, and they gonna kill somebody else's baby.
– Bernice Fitzpatrick, grandmother of 15-year old Demario Bailey during his funeral services held in Chicago, Illinois, 2014

This book is a tool for Black mothers to speak back to five spaces that have called them subjects (science), lazy (government), whores (mothering), apathetic (education), and degenerate (popular media). At the core *We Can Speak for Ourselves* is about vulnerability and claiming identities we were taught to despise (Cliff, 1980). Each woman takes space to say: I am not a 'baby mama'; I am Nikki, raising Nkrumah. I am not a 'Mammy'; I am Sonia, raising Selassie. I am not a belligerent black bitch; I am Maya, raising Mursi. Because this work demonstrates that Black women and mothers are human – and because of the human sacrifices being made in our streets *right now* – we must engage with Black *families* holistically. This book is a love letter to our children.

CIVIL RIGHTS

In 1955, Mamie Till Mobley opened the casket of her barely 14-year old son – Emmett Till – to reveal a face and body that had been beaten, shot, eyes gouged, and left in the Tallahatchie River weighed down by a cotton gin fan tied to his neck with barbed wire. Killing children was a tragedy so gripping, it arrested the attention of the nation and called forth our Civil Rights Movement – nationwide acts of civil disobedience and legislation which range from the Montgomery Bus Boycott (1955–1956) to the Voting Rights Act of 1965. To be clear, brutality against Black children was not new; children continuously experienced violence when ripped away from their families' arms, punished for learning, violated as sexual property, and hung just as their mothers and fathers were. Personal accounts, as well as cartoon images, have depicted Black children as "alligator bait" to promote dehumanization and fatal exploitation. As *No Fear for Freedom* author Kimberly Johnson (2013) recalls in her ethnographic studies of students and children from the Civil Rights era, it was common knowledge that Bull Connor – Public Safety Commissioner in Birmingham, Alabama – would parade his dog named "nigger" through residential streets to chase Black children (personal communication, 2014).

Placing youth at the center of the Civil Rights Movement – and naming those who have been attacked – has been lauded as a tactic to touch the humanity and heart of our nation. Children led the elders and filled the jails. They walked out of classrooms by the hundreds, marching 10 miles through Birmingham against fire hoses and attack dogs, and claimed it as the Children's Crusade. They desegregated schools across the country, which is beautiful immortalized by the Norman Rockwell image of 6-year old Ruby Bridges as she is escorted by deputy U.S. marshals against the backdrop of "nigger" and splattered tomatoes. They gave their lives – specifically four little girls named Addie Mae Collins, Cynthia Wesley, Carole Robertson, and Denise McNair who were murdered in a Birmingham church bombing and 14-year old George Stinney Jr.,[2] who was sentenced to the electric chair in South Carolina. They served as martyrs to reexamine our legal systems. There are still more children's names who are forgotten and unheard. As a nation's wealth is measured by how its children are educated and nurtured, we must take incredible pause when we bury a generation of them.

I invoke historical memory here because through the mid 1960's, elders and ancestors understood the power of youth engagement; in 2015, we again see youth at the forefront of action and as catalysts for social change. Where cities throughout the Deep South, particularly in Alabama – were major battlegrounds for civil rights gains, we now stand our ground in cities and states across the country: Chicago, Ferguson, Florida, Ohio, New York. I could not submit the final manuscript of this book – in this time – without acknowledging narratives of the past and naming the acts of violence, the role of social media, ideologies that continue to impact Black families, and provide tangible recommendations for further research.[3]

2015 BATTLE LINES

Moving through the Motherwork frame for this project, I opened each interview to understand the ways mothers communicate love to their children in an environment that calls for their protection and survival (Hill-Collins, 1990/2009). I asked direct questions like "what does it mean to protect Mursi?" or "Where do you feel like you take risks with Nkrumah?" Some responded with a simple "I don't know" and then began to think deeper. Others said they tell the truth no matter how uncomfortable it is. With respect to raising her (then) pre-teen son, Nikki prophetically recalled the statements she made to him:

> There is power in your voice. And pretty soon you are going to be 16 years old and 6'4" and they are not going to know you still have hug time with your mama, or that your mama has to remind you to zip up your pants in the morning. They are going to see you as a 6'4" young man and you are going to have to have a cool head about you.

These lessons – as mothers around the country have set forth – were shared just before the *new* open season on Black boys' and girls' lives.

At the time I began analyzing the data for this project, Trayvon Martin (February 5, 1995 – February 26, 2012) was murdered in Sanford, Florida. Eleven months later, Hadiya Pendleton (June 2, 1997 – January 29, 2013) was murdered in Chicago, Illinois – in the midst of 414 other murders in the city (CBS Chicago, 2014). "And as the President has said, we will never be able to eradicate every act of evil in this country but if we can save even one child's life we have an obligation to try when it comes to the scourge of gun violence" (The White House, Office of the Press Secretary, 2013). Any reasonable person will argue that one death is too many, yet we must be careful that the public and private conversations of the wars occurring in our cities potentially give way to dangerous distraction. It is not just an issue of gun control, but also of institutional and psychological warfare. For example, the misnomer "Chiraq" became popular to align the current wave of violence with the death toll by murder in Iraq. However, beyond the fact that this number is not a novel toll, markers such as "murder capital," (Desilver, 2014) signal a cry for military support and sets precedent for such action in our city when we the residents – families, teachers, elected/appointed officials, business owners, and children – are equipped to address these acts of violence ourselves. We witness tanks, armed guards, and discover loose grenades amongst scrap metal in our neighborhoods (Curry & Martinez, 2014; Klimas, 2012; Whitehead, 2013; Amin, 2015) alongside high-tension, public rhetoric that vacillates between "Black on Black crime" and "white vigilantism." This discourse operates as a game of political football when it's the lives of our children that are being thrown from hand to hand. And more often than not, Black women and mothers are on the community front lines of these crime scenes.

Near midnight on June 23, 2015, 34-year old Lucille Barnes was fatally shot near her home in Englewood – a neighborhood on the South Side of Chicago. The following Monday, Tamar Manasseh of "Mothers Against Senseless Killings" gathered with other women in the neighborhood referring to themselves as 'an army of mothers.' Manasseh states,

> If you're trying to shoot someone and we're out here, you're not getting off the block. This is about mothers reconnecting with children that haven't been mothered that much. Take away the guns, and they're just kids. When you start treating people like people again, and not like animals, people behave like people, parents behave like parents and the darndest thing happens: Kids start acting like kids and they stop shooting people. But it's a marathon and not a sprint. It's not just about the kids putting down the guns, it's about the kids never picking them up to begin with. A mother's love is selfless, annoying and always there. This is what mothers do best, get in the way. (Cholke, 2015b; Erbentraut, 2015)

DNAinfo reporter Cholke also noted "The group brought grills and hot dogs, but no police. The idea was to show in unmistakable terms that the message to would-be shooters is coming from within the community... [in the midst of casual conversations] they transmitted authority, vigilance and presence." Within that same week, during the July 4th holiday weekend when people make bets about the boom in homicides, there were none in Englewood. The Target Area Development Corp trained 300 residents on conflict resolution and, of course, the Army of Moms were present. "While a bigger police presence may have played a part, neighbors also give credit to community involvement" (Schulte, 2015).

These mothers apply restorative justice in a neighborhood not only plagued with violence and grenades but has garnered national attention as an area ripe for revitalization. In Fall 2014, developers broke ground for a Whole Foods market to be completed in 2016 along with Starbucks Coffee (Badger, 2014; Elejalde-Ruiz, 2015), which are clear signs of gentrification as noted by real estate mogul Spencer Rascoff (Kasperkevic, 2015; Rascoff, 2015). Welcoming major commercial businesses in neighborhoods such as these are a clear hallmark of segregation and displacement. Presenting options to buy $6 coffee drinks and $12 organic meals scream capitalism rather than community development. In fact, I posit that such moves deliberately destroy these communities because most families will not be able to afford such costs and in order for these businesses to thrive, they must be patronized by people with a house-hold income that is not currently present further asserting that the needs of the community are not a priority. Therefore, in line with Black families and parent involvement, the results reported by the University of Chicago Consortium on Chicago School Research raise major concerns (UCCSR, 2014).

The headline of a June 30, 2015 *DNAinfo* article states, "Survey ranks CPS teaching at the top, family involvement at the bottom." Given the findings of this project and current state of activism, this begs the question, "why?" According to a 2014 survey conducted by the University of Chicago Consortium on Chicago School Research with more than 104,000 teachers and 750,000 students across Illinois, "collaborative teaching" and "ambitious instruction" rated the highest while "family involvement" bottomed out. The participants were asked to rate their individual schools on the Five Essentials: ambitious instruction (teacher instruction is clear, engaging, academically challenging for students); effective leaders (the principal works with teachers to implement a shared vision for the school); collaborative teachers (teachers work together in order to promote professional growth); involved families (the entire school staff attempts to build external relationships connected to the school); and a supportive environment (a school is safe and supportive of students, teachers, and families).

> The report says it is possible that teachers and students were more negative on questions about safety in their community, trusting adults and neighborhood connections, which would have driven the rating down. 'A high level of crime and violence in some Chicago neighborhoods may undermine building social capital within these neighborhoods.' (Cholke, 2015a)

I am willing to argue that there is obviously *capital* in these neighborhoods as demonstrated by both the Army of Moms and the Whole Foods/Starbucks construction in Englewood – one of the most devastated communities in the city. The question is, how is this capital valued and leveraged to the benefit of the current and long-standing members of the community, i.e., Black mothers, fathers, and children? As Manasseh noted in their holiday weekend patrolling, "we were present and we really connected with residents of this community. Not just young people, but homeowners and people who have been there 30–40 years" (Schulte, 2015). These women operate under the mantra: "Our job is to love others without stopping to inquire whether or not they are worthy." Therefore, if the measurement of a *5 Essential* family involvement is "the entire school staff attempts to build external relationships connected to the school," where are they falling short?

Society is hard-pressed for remedies and solutions while many of us are simply trying to maintain enough balance to place one foot in front of the other. *We Can Speak for Ourselves,* timely in its exploration of Black mothers' ideologies, sets the table to further examine the proliferation of food desserts; access to medical care; redlining of both housing and entrepreneurship opportunities; quality education; and rampant, flagrant, police brutality or state-sanctioned violence – all recipes for terrorism against our Black children and the communities they call home. In her 2014 keynote lecture for the National Women's Studies Association annual conference, bell hooks reminds us

> If we only lay claim to those aspects of the system where we define ourselves as the oppressed and someone else as the oppressor, then we continually fail to see the larger picture… when we see how interlocking systems of domination work together, we are better able to discern the direction and renewed struggles social justice must take if our efforts to challenge and change these systems are to be most effective.

We may not have military authority and power, but we have voices and hearts and hands. We are not victims. We must tell our stories because to both *know* and *remember* ourselves is an act of decolonization (Love, 2015). The desperate plea of Bernice Fitzpatrick over the body of her slain grandson resonates loudly with the narratives within and beyond this work; we have to "love our own babies" and hence, we are a nation of mothers – speaking truth to power and healing. Again, this book is a love letter; a Black feminist, critical race, flat-foot truth tellin',[4] co-created call-to-action of self-awareness and tribute.

DOCUMENTING THE STREETS AND SOCIAL MEDIA QUALITY

To publish academic research about what is happening in the streets means you can't type fast enough. The sources that are deemed to hold "high standards to ensure quality" are also texts in which "ideas appear 10+ years after initiation" (Creswell, 2008, p. 95) such as encyclopedias and handbooks. More recent findings that are published in refereed journal articles are still deemed empirically sound as they are rigorously vetted as well. However, for this generation, it is the "indexed publications" and "early stage material" such as dissertations, online journals, and blogs, where "ideas appear first" (p. 95). We know this information matters because social media outlets such as Twitter and Facebook allow the general public, as well as major news outlets, and government institutions to deliver urgent, real-time messages ranging from natural disaster alerts, missing children reports, and civil disobedience protests. In fact, during the retrenchment of Black women images in media as discussed in Chapter 2, it was academic scholars, journalists, advocates, and organizations such as Princeton African American Studies professor Imani Perry (@ imaniperry); Wisconsin-Madison Urban Education Professor Gloria Ladson-Billings (@gjladson); political analyst and DNC Vice Chair Donna Brazile (@donnabrazile); NY Math educator Jose Vilson (@theJLV); anon feminist and family physician Jane Doe, MD (@DrJaneChi); African women's blog community – For Harriet (@forharriet); NC State History Professor Blair L. M. Kelley (@profblmkelley); and Philadelphia lawyer Wayne Bennett (@thefieldnegro), who all shared videos and article links that enabled me to cast a substantial net for the multiple discourses impacting the lives of Black women and mothers.

Mothers and police brutality.   Since the murder of Trayvon Martin, which gained incredible momentum and popular critical awareness through the circulation of a #iamtrayvon, the utility of social media has kept the ires of several issues burning, i.e., #BlackLivesMatter #BringBackOurGirls, and #SayHerName. Society is boiling with the uproar of so many lived experiences, that we must all redraft our knowledge around "high standards" and "quality" information. These relevant media sources are measured by unique visits, likes, and shares that can make a story 'go viral' which is a *global* litmus test. We are all witnesses and participants in transformative lived experiences and again, "the whole world watching."[5] Social media is a vibrant space – with the same trolls and biases we find in other sources – that we can not turn down or turn off. If we are earnestly plugged into the lives of our youth and the next generations, we must be plugged into their tools of communication.

On Dec 3, 2014, upon retweeting the grand jury decision of the non-indictment of Ferguson police officer Darren Wilson in the shooting death of Michael "Mike" Brown (May 20, 1996–August 9, 2014), Ijeoma Oluo, who identifies as a Black mother of two boys, fired off 30 tweets. These tweets were republished the following day as a digest in a *New York Magazine* article, "25 Activities Black People Should Avoid Around Cops" (Zavadski, 2014) with hyperlinks to all cases, which are provided in 25 notes at the end of this chapter.

> Don't play in the park with toy guns[6] and maybe they won't kill you. Don't ask for help after a car accident[7] and maybe they won't kill you. Don't wear a hoodie[8] and maybe they won't kill you. Don't cosplay with a toy sword[9] and maybe they won't kill you. Don't shop at WalMart[10] and maybe they won't kill you. Don't take the BART[11] and maybe they won't kill you. Don't ride your bike[12] and maybe they won't kill you. Don't reach for your cell phone[13] and maybe they won't kill you. Don't go to your friend's birthday party[14] and maybe they won't kill you. Don't sit on your front stoop[15] and maybe they

won't kill you. Don't "startle" them[16] and maybe they won't kill you. Don't "look around suspiciously"[17] and maybe they won't kill you. Don't walk on a bridge with your family[18] and maybe they won't kill you. Don't play "cops and robbers" with your buddies[19] and maybe they won't kill you. Don't work in a warehouse repairing instruments[20] and maybe they won't kill you. Don't stand in your grandma's bathroom[21] and maybe they won't kill you. Don't pray with your daughters in public[22] and maybe they won't kill you. Don't go to your bachelor party[23] and maybe they won't kill you. Don't have an ex boyfriend who might be a suspect[24] and maybe they won't kill you. Don't call for medical help for your sister[25] and maybe they won't kill her. Don't hang out in the park with your friends[26] and maybe they won't kill you. Don't get a flat tire[27] and maybe they won't kill you. Don't park in a fire lane[28] and maybe they won't kill you. Don't reach for your wallet[29] and maybe they won't kill you. Don't let your medical alert device go off[30] and maybe they won't kill you. I'm done for today. My heart can't handle any more.

The body cannot function without the mind. Chapter two of this book centers on the various attacks on Black women, which appeared to peak in 2011. Since that time, these attacks have become more vicious and deadly. Although mental health was not the focus of this study (and conventional research has often tied mental healthcare for Black women with poverty,) this scope must be widened. Because so many Black women fly under the mythical Superwoman banner, we must direct our attention to self-care and the quality of our mental health (Walton & Shepard Payne, 2015), and the stressors of this time cannot be overstated. Major barriers to mental health treatment are noted as denial, embarrassment, refusal of help, finances, fear, lack of knowledge, and hopelessness (Mental Health America). As timeless diagnoses such as post-partum, bipolar, acute anxiety, various addictions, and depression are dismissed as 'crazy,' 'you just do too much,' or 'take it to Jesus,' we contribute to our own destruction when we do not pause to seek help, and in-turn set devastating examples for our children. A quantitative study conducted in 2013 by Rahshida Atkins found among 208 single Black mothers between the ages of 18–45, that perceived stress, perceived racism, self-esteem, and anger provided an excellent explanation of depression in Black single mothers. This study aligns with the findings presented by McNeil, Harris-McKoy, Brantley, Fincham and Beach (2013), that among 189 Black mothers with children aged 7–14 years, a mother's perception of discrimination accounted for externalizing behaviors in their children "over and beyond that attributable to other stressful life events and socio-demographic variables… These results are consistent with the view that mothers' experience of greater discrimination leads to higher maternal depression" (p. 381).

Early in my career as a professor, I began working with a young Black woman who demonstrated a tremendous amount of drive and passion; however, her assignment grades seemed always to fall short of her major efforts. I reached out to her and in a one-on-one meeting she intimated her struggles as the primary parent for her teenage son and adolescent daughter, juggling 2.5 jobs, and the need to earn this degree as a token of something just for her – something that could ensure the promise of a career promotion and more for her family. Before the end of the quarter, she became ill with the stress and later shared that her son was scared for her life and begged her to take better care of herself.

She has never left my thoughts and compels me to consider the life of Sandra Bland – a 28-year old woman from Chicago whose case is too fresh to discuss in great detail but exposes too many wounds to completely overlook. In the mounting racial trauma that we are facing as a nation with respect to Dejerria Becton (McKinney, Texas) and the Charleston 9 – six women and three men – fatally shot during prayer service at the historic Emanuel African Methodist Episcopal Church, Bland sits at the base of the intersectional work we do with brutality against Black women and preservation of our mental health.

MAPS FOR FURTHER RESEARCH: IDEOLOGIES THAT CONTINUE TO IMPACT BLACK FAMILIES

Class and respect. This work addresses class with respect to the dominant discourse much more than within the mothers' narratives themselves. The mothers of this study discussed class as a fluidity of life rather than a fixed state. None of them discussed economic hardships they faced as mothers, which could have been latent when sharing stories of various means of family support. Even in the cases where they discussed neighborhood violence or living in public housing as young women, each narrative reflects both social and cultural movement beyond economic wealth, also known as "community cultural wealth" (Yosso, 2005, p. 69). The conventional markers of a low-working economic class, e.g., forms of government assistance, unemployment or no room for promotion, lack of medical care or services, poor schooling options for themselves or their children, were not present.

This is not to say these mothers' espouse a bootstraps-narrative – or one of meritocracy and blind privilege – but the everyday lives of their children are not muddied with the stressors of what their parents may have endured and/ or conquered; their children are not concerned with food, clothes, and shelter. Instead, the overarching themes of their everyday conversations are about holistic development that will exercise their talents, personal agency, and commitment to community. As women, each participant may have engaged with any number of the youthful exploits we all enjoy (and perhaps have been saved from); as mothers, each participant represents the middle-class woman who has come under scrutiny as a device of respectability politics. This device is issued as the standard for Black women, which conditions us to police for so-called bad behavior. Patricia Hill Collins (2004b) nods at the character of Clair Huxtable (as played by Phylicia Rashad on *The Cosby Show*) as "the new Black lady invented for middle- and upper-middle-class African American women. As a wife and mother, [she] was beautiful, smart, and sensuous. No cornrows, gum chewing, cursing, miniskirts, or plunging necklines (p. 139)." It is important to note as a controlling image, that very few Black mother characters who are featured on a major commercial network (i.e., American Broadcasting Company [ABC], Columbia Broadcasting System [CBS], and National Broadcasting Company [NBC])[31] are projected outside of this device.[32]

Further research must be conducted with a pool of women that cuts across and through a wider quantification of class. Why? So we don't confine motherhood to a set of definitions that work against our inherent sensibilities and lived experiences. This is necessary, so we do not recycle the good mother myth, which is largely hinged upon monetary provisions. We must discuss our value beyond our respective paychecks and bank accounts. In our work to embrace the Other, Deja, and Sapphire, we have to acknowledge that our willingness to do so – or not – speaks volumes about our individual concepts of *worth*, which "stem from cultural pathologies that [our devastation] can be altered through individual grit and exceptionally good behavior" (Coates, 2014, "A Difference of Kind, Not Degree," para. 9). Coates further asserts, "the kind of trenchant racism to which black people have persistently been subjected can never be defeated by making its victims more respectable."

In a 2014 feature article for *The Atlantic,* senior editor Ta-Nehisi Coates develops an extensive argument to support reparations for African Americans (H.R. 40 – 113th Congress), which rests upon the premise that the 250-plus-year atrocities of African enslavement and the material development of America *through* this extended trauma, be *acknowledged.* My intent for introducing this is not to redirect the conversation toward reparations, as much as it both acknowledge and understand the ties between white economic class, Black bodies, Black families, and white supremacy.

> The wealth accorded America by slavery was not just in what the [Africans] pulled from the land but in the [Africans] themselves... Loans were taken out for purchase, to be repaid with interest. Insurance policies were drafted against the untimely death of a[n African] and the loss of potential profits. [African] sales were taxed and notarized. The vending of the black body and the sundering of the black family became an economy unto themselves, estimated to have brought in tens of millions of dollars to antebellum America. ("The Ills That Slavery Frees Us From" section, para. 8)

He later writes, "if Thomas Jefferson's genius matters, then so does his taking of Sally Heming's body" ("We Inherit Our Ample Patrimony" section, para. 14). This elucidates the connection that our Black bodies *are* capital and why race can hardly be severed from class. Both Clair Huxtable and Deja – as well as all of their children – are subject to the terrorism of housing discrimination, education apartheid, and state-sanctioned violence. When bell hooks (2014) spoke of the murder of

John Crawford, or the WalMart killing as she called it, she admitted that her position has been a bit controversial – not because she was speaking against racism, but because she believes his murder had a great deal to do with his age and the consumption of post-race propaganda:

> That what Black man living in the violence of this white supremacist culture, could have that kind of faith in the humanity of white people and they had *no* faith in him… *young* Black people, more than any other group, young People of Color, are living in the cognitive dissonance of being told on one hand that racism has ended, and on one hand *trusting in that, enough* to believe that they can call forth a humanity in white people – white *aggressors*, white supremacists – that is just not there. I think these are really insane times around cognitive dissonance, around domination of the many, many forms that white supremacy takes. Because one of the things that we don't talk about as Black people… I mean there's a reason why sooo many young Black people are obsessed with wealth. Because they believe that *wealth* can take them out of the circumstance of danger – that they could finally be "free" – if they had the money.

To be clear, poverty is real; it is not a socialist construct cooked up by the unmotivated and undeserving peoples within our society. However, in our democratic system, there are to be structures for mobility. For the privileged, class mobility is inherited or willed; for some, class mobility exists within a hidden curriculum; for others, it is tangled in the crosshairs of racism and discrimination or must take a backseat to check-to-check survival. Moreover, just because you can barely budget a government-mandated living wage does not mean you are immoral or criminal. On the converse, just because you are part of a higher tax bracket does not mean you have stronger values / or forgot the values of your elders and ancestors. The issue here is two-fold: amassing and sustaining economic wealth in addition to accessing and creating knowledge that cultivates self-worth. This is why when I asked Maya why didn't she move after witnessing so much violence – having to cross police tape to enter her home – she refers to their 3-flat and says: "we are here. Upstairs. Downstairs… Family is that unconditional net of love that takes you through the good, the bad and the ugly… No matter what is going on out there." A building "full of [us]" has been more important to her above all else. In the construction of wealth, let us persist with telling the narratives of every *building*.

Black fathers. Another parent that was consistently involved at SSCES was James.[33] He was a police officer, and I remember him attending various meetings and events; I would also see him in church and around the city. Running into him so often reminded me of the narratives you hear about Black education before desegregation – that the teachers and parents were so immersed in the same community, a child could hardly draw the line between home and school. James was very present; however, he was the only father I had immediate access to as a member of The Beacons – which was a participant limitation of this study. He, like most other parents, had a grueling responsibility of managing time – especially as a civil servant, his time was often not his own. Therefore, as much as I wanted to engage with him for this project, it was not possible for that season. Surely his participation in this study would've provided a different shape and ultimately I chose to stand firm in the rationale that the work and voices of Black mothers' must be shared in the conversation of parent involvement especially because it is mothers that are conventionally privileged with the responsibility of 'showing up to the school.' It is for this same reason that James and so many fathers I have interacted with throughout the years demand space for their narratives as well.

While there is much scholarship, activism, art, and legislation concerning the atrocities Black men face in America against their physical bodies and psyche, there is a narrow space to recognize their fatherhood, which is deemed both a personal luxury and a social abomination. As various controlling images of Black women were noted in Chapter 2 of this work, the image of the "Black Buck" as both a virile breeder and violent, sexual predator, have perhaps been more consistent and persistent than Mammy. The humanity of Black men was so thoroughly destroyed that the anguish of being separated from his children has not been acknowledged as a viable response. More injury to the soul was the birth of a child from any sort of union of this sort – another life disregarded as another means of literal currency and trade. "In a time when telecommunications were primitive and blacks lacked freedom of movement, the parting of black families was a kind of murder" (Coates, 2014, "The Ills That Slavery Frees Us From" section, para. 12). I argue that this parting of the Black family was *exactly* murder.

The violence our ancestors endured – the loss of their own bodies – as Coates (2014) notes, created an abyss of fear for our children but also unchartered spaces for love. While earnestly trying to wrap and tighten the epilogue of this manuscript (I am so grateful to the editors and typesetters for responding to the multiple revisions,) my body ached with the unyielding news reports of all the lost Black bodies. I stepped away from social media and back to the comfort of paperbacks, excited to read the latest work of Coates (2015) – a letter to his 15-year old son. My soul stirred when reading his reflection of his son's birth:

> We'd summoned you out of ourselves, and you were not given a vote. If only for that reason, you deserved all the protection we could muster. Everything else was subordinate to this fact. If that sounds like a weight, it shouldn't. The truth is that I owe you everything I have. Before you, I had my questions but nothing beyond my own skin in the game, and that was really nothing at all because I was a young man, and not yet clear of my own human vulnerabilities. But I was grounded and domesticated by the plain fact that should I now go down, I would not go down alone. (p. 66)

Coates speaks of love for his child that is palpable. This love is hard-won and often too urgent to pause, celebrate, let it soak in and nurture us all, so we can grab and share even more love. Moreover, when we hear of parents' love that is reverent and "vulnerable," we look to mothers; controlling images of Black fathers shift our sight away from the incredible heart-work they do every day.

Maya, Nikki, and Sonia talk about the roles of the fathers in their children's lives as critical to their development while they are both inside and outside of their respective homes. Because we understand the traumatic devastation the Maafa has on the Black family, the father's narrative can not be minimized. We must create more projects that counter dominant/controlling narratives, which reduce Black fathers to DNA results and television punchlines where audiences scream: "you are not the father!" We must create and seek out more projects – such as the Dovetail Project – that unearth, enrich, and celebrate the full humanity of Black fathers. We must explore and embrace the entire village.

Little brothers and sisters.   From mothers to fathers, we come full circle to our children. I began my education work in 1998 as a tutor and mentor with CPS. I primarily – often exclusively – worked with boys. However, in my last position as an afterschool director I began to focus on the needs of adolescent Black girls. The environment often created a tension steeped in self-identity, hormones, and academic ambition. I created and facilitated peer groups for the girls, recognizing some of the same questions, arguments and concerns I had 20 years prior. There were no magic recipes – I worked tirelessly with other Black girls and women to build ideas and projects that we either had or wanted to have when we were growing up. They kept me buried in ways to grow us as a group, continually feed their hunger, and build upon their resiliency. I found bridges with the community works Project Butterfly and SistaStrong; I culled wisdom from the research and creative works of Rebecca Carroll (1997), Iris Jacob (2002), Kiri Davis (2005) and Venus Evans-Winters (2005/2011). They made me go to graduate school, and I felt like they were doing the work with me. "I entered Chapel Hill with two goals: one, learn how to teach teachers and two, acquire and create tools to facilitate the development of positive identities of Black girls (because that's what good educated Black girls do – give back)" (Sankofa Waters, 2015).

Mamie Till Mobley, Wanda Johnson, Annette Nance-Holt, Lucia McBath, Anjanette Albert, Sabrina Fulton, Cleopatra Cowley-Pendleton, and Leslie McSpadden bring the words of Audre Lorde (1977/2007) back to us. Reflecting upon her terminal diagnosis she recalls "…what I most regretted were my silences. To question or to speak I believe could have meant pain, or death. But we all hurt in so many different ways, all the time, and pain will either change or end" (p. 41). We witnessed the final silence of their children's deaths as a spile into their hearts; what has poured out is action and national mobilization of youth.

Blog entry for January 29, 2013. I got a call that no one ever wants to get: "Hadiya was shot and it doesn't look good." I listened as my friend and Hadiya's former 4th/5th grade teacher told me Hadiya was dismissed early because of midterm exams and was assembled with a group of students when someone randomly shot into the crowd.

Hadiya was in my first class of afterschool students at my first "big girl" job. She along with my 2nd and 4th graders brought me full circle to Black feminism, urban education, and myself. She was incredibly instrumental in pushing me to develop Sunflower Seeds Studio. She had a righteous awareness that I was blessed to witness when she was just 9-years old. With her quick wit, ceaseless questions, sensitivity, and independent spirit, she held a disarming smile that she inherited from both her mother and father and dimples she shared with her little brother. Her parents were fiercely protective and loving; I was honored they invited me into their home as an othermother. It feels cruel to write all of this in past tense. I was certain the world would bare [sic] witness to Hadiya's light (we believe this about all of our children, right?) but I ABSOLUTELY did not believe it would be like this – to be extinguished after only 15 years.

The Chicago Tribune, CNN, Ebony, MSNBC and headlines across the world reported "Girl who performed at Obama inaugural events slain on South Side." Yes, Hadiya was an Honor Roll student, a volleyball player, a majorette; she is a part of history – nationally and locally. And as if my heart could not sink any further, one local news reporter found it important to note: *She was not affiliated with any gangs* (as was clearly marked for 15-year old Cornelius German who was murdered three months later, also near the Obamas' home [Bowean & Sweeney, 2013]). Several reporters made efforts to provide more statements and phrases such as, *no previous arrest record, promising,* and *traveling to Paris.* Hadiya was the 42nd person murdered in Chicago during just the first 30 days of the year; however, her death was the first to be publically mourned. The language of the reports seemed to give residents permission to grieve her death because she earned it by being a "traditional student" (Watson, 2009) – not one "at-risk" (U.S. Department of Education, 2006). Nevertheless, the tragedy of her death suggests that risk factors cannot be sole quantitative calculations in a major city with complicated residential histories, unemployment rates, and ill-distributed youth resources. Klyn Jones, Hadiya's friend who held her hand that day in Vivian Harsh Park, later stated: "she would really want all of us to smile and know that she's in a better place, because heaven is a lot safer than Chicago" (Balde, Releford, & Lutz, 2013). When the Chicago news ticks on and we learn about Endia Martin (May 26, 1999 – April 28, 2014) and Gakirah "Lil Snoop" Barnes (1997 – April 11, 2014) it appears that Klyn's raw message carries too much truth.

Every day we work with those who are products of technology, crack, Hip Hop, "reality" media, and the cultural mores (King & Mitchell, 1990; Ladner, 1995) of our ancestors and elders. It is important that we raise our voices and hands with them to claim #BlackLivesMatter, not just so the world knows, but so each of them understands this as a daily, personal truth. This is the function of culturally relevant education, which demands that we unremittingly stimulate high expectations of excellence four our children, cultivate full competence of their cultural wealth, and create knowledge that critiques social order (Ladson-Billings, 1995). There are amazing spaces across the country where this is occurring – especially with respect to Hip Hop education. In her 2012 work, *Hip Hop's Li'l Sistas Speak,* Bettina Love notes,

> I can remember sitting in a class as a teenager asking myself whether anyone cared about what was going on in my community besides my friends and me. I recall thinking to myself that KRS-One knew more about me, my community, and my history as an African American than did my teachers, regardless of race, whom I saw everyday. (p. 104)

This passage lends itself to one approach: "Teaching through a Hip Hop-inspired pedagogical and media literacy approach is culturally responsive pedagogy with possibilities for social action in that teaching through a culturally relevant framework is restructuring classroom politics" (p. 103; Emdin, 2010). From the Dream Defenders based out of Florida (http://dreamdefenders.org), to Black Youth Project 100 based out of Chicago (http://byp100.org), and Radical Monarchs based out of LA, our children – little brothers and sisters – are our hope and our promise. We write love letters to our children, little brothers and little sisters (Love, 2012; Coates, 2015; Whitehead, 2015), especially in times of war, because this is how we speak truth to power.

CHALLENGE

Not one person can deny the heart drop and belly ache of a mother sentenced to five years for enrolling their child in a better school system; the mother who faces a 3-year jail sentence for walking across the street when an over-medicated, partially blind, drunk driver killed her 4-year old child; swallowing the knowledge that coming home from school may end in death; being fined for child abuse simply because you are unmarried; or having to claim your child who lay in a morgue as John Doe after going out for Skittles and iced tea. No one can stomach these tragedies. Much less a mother. A mother who expects her child to surpass her own dreams.

There are many of us who are specially equipped with a range of talents and tools to attack and dismantle these perpetual strongholds. We must challenge what it means to be "at-risk" think critically about what it means to live "in an urban community," what systems are we complicit which perpetuate the poor, and who we deem so-called worthy of our blood, sweat, and tears. True risk, is fearlessness. Consider the words of Paulo Freire: "...the oppressed, who have adapted to the structure of domination in which they are immersed, and have become resigned to it, are inhibited from waging the struggle for freedom so long as they feel incapable of running the risk it requires" (Freire, 1970/2000, p. 47). We must exorcise our fear and leverage our privileges unto the least of these – understanding our trajectories could have easily been altered without the supports that have been graciously provided for us. Whether it is a child who subscribes to the rhythmic fallacies of Lil Wayne and Chief Keef or a child who is in a band for Obama, we have all been enlisted to be – as Dr. King noted – "drum majors for justice" (Dr. Martin L. King, Jr., 1968). We have to be sure we are moving beyond the texts. Of course I recognize the irony of stating this within a text, but this work documents *action*.

I challenge Sociologists, Educators, and Qualitative Researchers to own our multiple identities. Embrace the intersectionality within ourselves and make room for the unexpected. Ask questions that we do not know the answers to. Embed reciprocity in *every* project. Check our egos at the door. Imagine the world as a research site for change. Critique social order. Plant seeds in small and local corners. Take our gloves off. Refrain from regurgitating data. Ask before we identify. Dance with our participants and students, even when they are not around. Set high expectations. Destroy the binaries. Employ the use of culturally relevant lenses. Revisit ideas. Create new languages.

I challenge Black women, mothers, and feminists to continue telling our stories. Talk to one another so that we heal, pass wisdom, and hold one another accountable. Forgive one another. Forgive ourselves. Release the Superwoman myth and understand there is no "right" or "wrong" way to be exactly who we are and we will change again. Let our "no's" be "no's" and our "yes's" be "yes's" – without apology. Realize our own mothers as full women so that we may understand ourselves as the same. Be bold. Exercise self-care and therapy. Remove the language of 'single' and embrace our villages. Love our partners fiercely. Scaffold our children – even the ones not birthed to us. Be unafraid to love; it is a dangerous act. Journal your thoughts and claim them as poetry. Create new languages.

I challenge Community and Social Justice advocates to serve *all*. Take directions with humility. Trust the shoulders we stand on. Honor the backs that have been broken. Let the youth speak. Do not take no for an answer. Understand that each day gives us 1440 opportunities to breathe, laugh, scream, teach, learn, and choose our own adventures. Tithe into small businesses. Visualize the world we fight for. Don't watch the clock. Cut with truth; seal with hope. Create new languages.

I challenge each of us, as I challenge myself.

– Mandou Billye Sankofa Waters, August 2015

NOTES

[1] Transformative essay written by Michelle Cliff (1985/1995) regarding the intersectional identities of race, class, gender, sexuality, religion, age, and nationalism.

[2]   George Stinney Jr. (October 21, 1929 – June 16, 1944) was the youngest person – 14-years old – to be executed in the United States in the 20th century. He was charged with first-degree murder of two White girls aged 11 and 8, with no physical evidence and only a 10-minute deliberation of an all-White jury. It is reported that he used a bible as a booster to sit in the electric chair. His conviction was vacated December 17, 2014 – 70 years after his murder (Robertson, 2014).

[3]   Content updates prior to the Epilogue include noteworthy transitions within the Chicago Public Schools and select lecture notes from bell hooks' National Women's Studies Association 2014 Annual Conference keynote address.

[4]   See *Flat-footed Truths: Telling Black Women's Lives* (Bell-Scott, 1998).

[5]   The anti-war chant of 10,000 demonstrators outside the Chicago Hilton Hotel during the 1968 Democratic National Convention, which was televised to nearly 83 million Americans (Marcus, n.d.).

[6]   Tamir Rice, 12 years old (c. 2002–2014).

[7]   Jonathan Ferrell, 24 years old (1988–2013).

[8]   Jordan Baker, 26 years old (1987–2014).

[9]   Darrien Hunt, 22 years old (2014).

[10]   John Crawford, 22 years old (2014).

[11]   Oscar Grant, III, 22 years old (2009).

[12]   Dante Parker, 36 years old (2014).

[13]   Travis McNeill, 28 years old (2011).

[14]   Kimani Gray, 16 years old (2013).

[15]   Bernard Monroe, 73 years old (2009).

[16]   Akai Gurley, 28 years old (2014).

[17]   Steven Eugene Washington, 27 years old (2010).

[18]   James Brissette, 17 years old and Ronald Madison, 40 years old (2005).

[19]   Nicholas Heyward, 13 years old (1994).

[20]   Ousmane Zongo, 43 years old (2003).

[21]   Ramarley Graham, 18 years old (2012).

[22]   Manual Loggins, Jr., 31 years old (2012).

[23]   Sean Bell, 23 years old (2006).

[24]   Tarika Wilson, 26 years old (2008).

[25]   Shereese Francis, 30 years old (2012).

[26]   Rekia Boyd, 22 years old (2012).

[27]   Tyisha Miller, 19 years old (1998).

[28]   Danroy Henry, Jr., 20 years old (2010).

[29]   Amadou Diallo, 23 years old (1999).

[30]   Kenneth Chamberlain, Sr., 68 years old (2011).

[31]   I only highlight these major networks because of their historical and national reach into the "everyday" household across the country – prior to the expansion of cable and specialty networks.

[32]   To date, the roster includes Diahann Carroll in the title role of *Julia* (Baker) which aired on NBC five months after the assassination of Dr. Martin Luther King and ran for three seasons. She is followed by Florida Evans in 1974 (Ester Rolle, five seasons with CBS); Mary Jenkins in 1985 (Marla Gibbs, five season with NBC); Harriett Winslow in 1989 (Jo Marie Payton, five seasons with CBS); Aunt Viv in 1990 (Janet Hubert, 3 seasons with NBC); and Janet "Jay" Kyle (Tisha Campbell-Martin, five seasons on ABC).

[33]   This parent was assigned a pseudonym of James (Baldwin).

PARTICIPANTS

(at time of initial meeting through the course of interviews)

Name	Age	Interview Location	Interview Duration	Grade School	Marital Status	Occupation	Child(ren)
Maya	Late 40	Home	3.66	Catholic	Single	Undisclosed	Mursi
Nikki	Late 30	Home	2	Suburban	Single	Admin	Nkrumah
Carolyn	Late 30	Restaurant	1	Catholic	Married/ Separated	Admin	Kanuri
							Khoi
Jill	Mid 40	Coffee Shop	1.5	Private	Undisclosed	Teacher	Jola
							Undisclosed
Sonia	Mid 30	Phone	2	Public	Married	Undisclosed	Sundiata
							Selassie
							Undisclosed

INITIAL INTERVIEW GUIDE

1. Background information
   Probes:

   - Tell me about living in Chicago.
   - Tell me about your schooling experiences.
   - How were parents involved in your school?

2. [School Choice] Why did you decide to enroll your child/ren in this school?

   - What were the schooling options for your children?
   - How did you gather information about school options?
   - What criteria did you use in school selection?
   - How did you ultimately decide on a school for your child/ren?

3. [School Grounds] What have been your interactions with the school faculty and staff?

   - What were your interactions with your school of choice prior to enrollment?
   - What have been your interactions with this school post enrollment?
   - What have you observed about the interaction between other parents and school staff?
   - To what extent do you feel integrated into the school community?

4. [Collaborative Resources] What have been your interactions with parents/other children?

   - What are your interactions with students within/outside of the school?
   - What are your interactions with parents within/outside of the school?
   - What have you observed about the involvement of other parents in the school?
   - How comfortable do you feel with being actively involved at this school?

5. [Direct Involvement] How have you been directly involved with the school?

   - What resources are available to you as a parent?
   - How are you used as a resource?
   - What are the current opportunities for you to be involved with the school?
   - How are you informed of school activities and opportunities for involvement?
   - In what ways are you/would you like to be involved with the school? your child/ren?

- How are you encouraged and equipped by the school to be involved?
- How are you encouraged and equipped by the community to be involved?

6. [Future] What are your future plans with your child/ren and the direction of the school?

- What are your achievement goals for your child/ren?
- How are these goals facilitated by the school?
- How are you encouraged to work collaboratively toward these goals?
- What are you plans for current and future involvement with the school?

SECOND INTERVIEW GUIDE

Hill-Collins uses the term motherwork which "can be done on behalf of one's own biological children, or for the children of one's own racial ethnic community, or to preserve the earth for those children who are yet unborn" (2004a, p. 48). This includes:

1. *Women-Centered Networks (WCN)* which are described as a community of mothers, grandmothers, sisters, aunts, cousins [or neighbors] responsible for taking care of the children. Because of the historical value of WCN, many of these women grow to gain "a reputation for never turning away a needy child" (Hill-Collins, 1990/2009, p. 198).

   - How do you define mother?
   - Who are you mother to?
   - How did you come to the decision of Motherhood?
   - What did you learn from your mother?

2. *Mothers and Daughters* describes the ways mothers communicate love in an environment that calls for their protection and survival.

   - How is raising [] different from how you were raised?
   - What does it mean to protect []?
   - Where do you feel like you take risks with []?

3. *Community Othermothers and Political Activism* describes "mothering of the mind" which demands education to be used in a socially responsible way.

   - How is [] equipped to make decisions?
   - How are you preparing [] to enter the world?

4. *Motherhood as a Symbol of Power explores* issues of class, the dumbing down of Black women's work and the work of community women who are "nameless in scholarly texts, yet everyone in their neighborhoods knows their names" (1990/2009, p. 208).

   - Are there expectations of you as a Black mother?
   - Are there stereotypes you feel like you have to deny or speak against as a Black mother?

5. *The View from the Inside* describes mothering as a "fundamentally contradictory institution" (1990/2009, p. 211) and shares the narratives of Black mothers. These tenets provide a framework that employ an intersectional approach, engaging gender with race and class, to shift the prevailing motherhood discourse.

- Discussion of court cases

GLOSSARY OF PSEUDONYMS

Carolyn M. Rodgers (1940–2010)

Black Arts Movement Poet. Essayist. Critic. Lecturer. Teacher. Rodgers studied with Pulitzer Prize-winning poet Gwendolyn Brooks and formed the Organization of Black American Culture. She wrote poetry that grappled with issues of Black identity and culture in the late 1960s and quickly became recognized for delving into the problems and challenges facing Black women. Her poetry was collected in volumes including "Paper Soul," "Songs of a Black Bird" and "How I got ovah." She was inducted into the Gwendolyn Brooks Center for Black Literature and Creative Writing at Chicago State University International Literary Hall of Fame for Writers of African Descent in 2009 (Gates & McKay, 1997; Jenson, 2010).

Deja K. Taylor (c. 1990)

Writer. Performer. Mentor. Deja is a major voice in the new generation of Hip Hop/theatre female poets. She was recently featured in Russell Simmons' HBO production of *Brave New Voices* for her poem "Ode to the Female MC" which launched her into the public eye. The Chicago native has successfully headlined an international tour: *Beautiful Grind,* and is currently developing a one-woman show manifesto: *Free Deja Taylor.* She continues to perform and work as a teaching-artist in schools across the country. For more information, visit: http://dejavoodootaylor.blogspot.com

Haile Selassie I (1892–1975)

Selassie was Ethiopia's regent from 1916 to 1930 and Emperor of Ethiopia from 1930 to 1974. He was the heir to a dynasty that traced its origins to the 13th century and from there, by tradition back to King Solomon and Queen Makeda, Empress of Axum, known in the Abrahamic tradition as the Queen of Sheba. Haile Selassie is a defining figure in both Ethiopian and African history ("Haile Selassie", n.d.).

James Baldwin (1924–1987)

Poet. Playwright. Novelist. Bold advocate and critic of human rights. Global citizen. It is perhaps easier to note what Baldwin did *not* do for Blacks and

American culture as a whole. His first collection of work *The Fire Next Time* (1963) has been hailed his greatest but that does not subtract from his genius; his physical work spans four decades, while his holistic legacy extends lightyears beyond. "All of James Baldwin's writings bear some stamp of his assertion that 'all art is a kind of confession,' that all artists, if they are to survive, are forced, at last, to tell the whole story, to 'vomit the anguish up.' But in Baldwin's work, such confession was not merely a self-indulgent form of personal catharsis. With elegance and artfulness, he pierced the historic block in America's racial consciousness by linking the most intimate areas of his own experience with the broadest questing of national and global destiny." (Gates & McKay, 1997, pp. 1650–1651)

Jill Scott (1972)

Singer. Poet. Actress. Philanthropist. With initial dreams of becoming a high school teacher, Jill Scott began her performing career as a spoken word artist, appearing at live poetry readings. She is a self-taught vocalist that listened to Leontyne Price, Sarah Vaughn, and Millie Jackson while working odd-jobs including hotel cleaning and construction sites to sustain herself before receiving major public recognition. She has since launched a highly-successful, multi-platinum selling career earning both Grammy and NAACP Image Awards. In addition to her music career, she has trained as an actress garnering lead roles such as Mama Ramotswe in the BBC/HBO series *The No. 1 Ladies' Detective Agency* based on the Botswana/South African novels of the same name. In 2003, she began the Blues Babe Foundation and in 2005 she published her first collection of poetry: *The Moments, the Minutes, the Hours*. For more information, visit: http://www.jillscott.com

Jola

The Jola (or Diola) are an ethnic group primarily located in Senegal, The Gambia, and Guinea-Bissau. Primary languages spoken are Jola and Kriol. Jolas are herbal medicine practitioners with a musical and rice-centered civilization ("The Gambia", n.d.).

Kanuri

Kanuri peoples include several subgroups and identify by different names in some regions; their primary locations are northeastern Nigeria, southeast Niger, western Chad and northern Cameroon. They have traditionally been sedentary, engaging in farming, fishing, trade, and salt processing. Kanuri remains a major language in southeastern Niger, and some 3 million Kanuri speakers live in Nigeria. For more information, visit: http://www.africanholocaust.net/peopleofafrica

Khoi

The Khoi-san are one of the eldest ethnic groups in Southern Africa. The Khoi-san languages are noted for their click consonants, which have no alphabetical equivalent in any script. Today many of the San live in parts of the Kalahari Desert where they are better able to preserve much of their culture. For more information, visit: http://www.africanholocaust.net/peopleofafrica

Kwame Nkrumah (1909–1972)

Nkrumah was the leader of Ghana and its predecessor state, the Gold Coast, from 1952 to 1966. Overseeing the nation's independence from British colonial rule in 1957, Nkrumah was the first President of Ghana and the first Prime Minister of Ghana. An influential 20th-century advocate of Pan-Africanism, he was a founding member of the Organization of African Unity and was the winner of the Lenin Peace Prize in 1963 ("Kwame Nkrumah", n.d.).

Mansa Sundiata Keita (c. 1217–c. 1255)

Keita founded the Mali Empire and celebrated as a hero of the Mandinka people of West Africa. The epic of Sundiata is primarily known through oral tradition, transmitted by generations of Mandinka griots (oral historians). He is well-known for creating a stable and peaceful government that laid the foundation for the prosperous rule of other leaders for subsequent centuries. For more information, visit: http://www.africanlegends.info

Maya Angelou/Marguerite Ann Johnson (1928–2014)

Poet. Memoirist. Novelist. Educator. Dramatist. Producer. Actress. Historian. Filmmaker. Civil Rights activist. As a young mother, she supported her son by working as a waitress and cook; however, her passion for music, dance, performance, and poetry would soon take center stage. In 1970, she began work on the book that would become *I Know Why the Caged Bird Sings*, which was published to international acclaim and enormous popular success. The list of her published verse, non-fiction, and fiction now includes more than 30 bestselling titles. Dr. Angelou has served on two presidential committees, was awarded the Presidential Medal of Arts in 2000, the Lincoln Medal in 2008, and has received three Grammy Awards. She has received over 30 honorary degrees and is the Reynolds Professor of American Studies at Wake Forest University (Gates & McKay, 1997). For more information, visit: http:// www.mayaangelou.com

Mursi

The Mursi (or Murzu) are an African nomadic cattle herder people located in the Omo valley in southwestern Ethiopia, close to the Sudanese border. The estimated population of the Mursi is around 3,900. Surrounded by mountains and three rivers, the home of the Mursi is one of the most isolated regions of the country. The Mursi tongue is also called Mursi. For more information, visit: http://www.africanholocaust.net/peopleofafrica

Nikki Giovanni/Yolande Cornelia Giovanni (b. 1943)

Poet. Writer. Commentator. Activist. Educator. She published her first book of poetry, *Black Feeling Black Talk* in 1968 and within the next year published a second book, thus launching her career as a writer and was dubbed the "Princess of Black Poetry." Over the course of more than three decades of publishing and lecturing, she has authored over 30 books for adults and children and her honors have been steady and plentiful. Giovanni is the recipient of some 25 honorary degrees and is a University Distinguished Professor at Virginia Tech in Blacksburg, Virginia (Gates & McKay, 1997). For more information, visit: http://nikki-giovanni.com

Sonia Sanchez/Wilsonia Benita Driver (b. 1934)

Poet. Mother. Professor. National and International lecturer on Black Culture and Literature, Women's Liberation, Peace and Racial Justice. Sonia Sanchez is the author of over 16 books in addition to being a contributing editor to *Black Scholar* and *The Journal of African Studies.* She has performed her work on six of the seven continents and has lectured at over 500 universities and colleges in the United States. She was the first Presidential Fellow at Temple University where she also held the Laura Carnell Chair in English (Gates & McKay, 1997). For more information, visit: http://soniasanchez.net/bio/

REFERENCES

Adiche, C. (2012, March). *To instruct and delight: A case for realist literature.* Lecture conducted at the Commonwealth Lecture, London, England.

Alexander, R. C., McNeal, M., Mwangola, M. S., & Zabriskie, Q. M. E. (2007). The quilt: Towards a twenty-first-century Black feminist ethnography. *Performance Research, 3*(12), 54–83.

Ali, S. (1989). *The Blackman's guide to understanding the Blackwoman.* Philadelphia, PA: Civilized Publications.

Amin, R. (2015, January 27). Bomb squad investigating report of grenades in car in Englewood. *The Chicago Sun Times.* Retrieved from http://chicago.suntimes.com/news/7/71/324196/ bomb-squad-investigating-report-grenades-car-englewood

Anderson, J. D. (1988). *The education of Blacks in the south 1860–1935.* Chapel Hill, NC: University of North Carolina Press.

Andrews, H. (2011, April 22). Good education is a right, not a crime. *The Root.* Retrieved from http://www.theroot.com/views/good-education-right-not-crime

Ani, M. (1980). *Let the circle be unbroken: The implications of African spirituality in the diaspora.* New York, NY: Nkonimfo Publications.

Ani, M. (1994). *Yurugu: An Afrikan-centered critique of European cultural thought and behavior.* Trenton, NJ: Africa World Press.

Atkins, R. (2015). Depression in Black single mothers. *Western Journal of Nursing Research, 37*(6), 812–830. doi:10.1177/0193945914528289

Austin, R. (2003). Sapphire bound! In A. K. Wing (Ed.), *Critical race feminism* (2nd ed., pp. 301–308). New York, NY: New York Press.

Badger, E. (2015, November 14). Why whole foods is moving into one of the poorest neighborhoods in Chicago. *The Washington Post.* Retrieved from http://www.washingtonpost.com/blogs/wonkblog/wp/2014/11/14/why-whole-foods-is-moving-into-one-of-the-poorest-neighborhoods-in-chicago/

Balde, L., Releford, M., & Lutz, B. J. (2013, January 30). Teen performer at inaugural events fatally shot in Chicago. *NBC Chicago.* Retrieved from http://www.nbcchicago.com/news/local/Chicago-Teen-Performer-At-Inaugural-Events-Fatally-Shot--189007181.html

Barton, A. C., Drake, C., Perez, J. G., St. Louis, K., & George, M. (2004). Ecologies of parental engagement in urban education. *Educational Researcher, 33*(4), 3–12.

Bell-Scott, P. (Ed.). (1998). *Flat-footed truths: Telling Black women's lives.* New York, NY: Henry Holt and Company.

Bluestein, G. (2012, April 17). Raquel Nelson fights murder charges in son's jaywalking death in Georgia. *Huffington Post.* Retrieved from http://www.huffingtonpost.com/2012/04/17/raquel-nelson-jaywalking-death-charges-georgia_n_1432177.html?

Bowean, L., & Sweeney, A. (2013, April 24). Mom finds son, 15, slain: I'm questioning my faith. *The Chicago Tribune.* Retrieved from http://articles.chicagotribune.com/2013-04-24/news/ chi-4-shot-in-englewood-20130422_1_gang-members-hadiya-pendleton-harsh-park

Boylorn, R. (2013a). Blackgirl blogs, auto/ethnography, and crunk feminism. *Liminalities: A Journal of Performance Studies, 9*(2), 73–82.

Boylorn, R. (2013b). *Sweetwater: Black women and narratives of resilience.* New York, NY: Peter Lang.

Boylorn, R. (2013c, September 30). *Mama's feminism* [Blog]. Retrieved from http://www.crunkfeministcollective.com/2013/09/30/mamas-feminism/

Brice Heath, S. (1983). *Words at work and play: Three decades in family and community life.* Cambridge, England: Cambridge University Press.

Brown, S. L. (2014, November 18). Untold story of Black fatherhood. *Colorlines.* Retrieved from http://colorlines.com/archives/2014/11/fatherhood.html

Byrne, J. (2012, October 12). Departing Brizard to get full year's salary. *Chicago Tribune.* Retrieved from http://articles.chicagotribune.com/2012-10-12/news/chi-departing-brizard-to-get-full-years-salary-20121012_1_brizard-school-closings-education-president-david-vitale

Carlton, P. E. R., Rhodes, B., & Brown, C. (2011). Unpacking the CRT in negotiating white science. *Cultural Studies of Science Education, 6*(4), 951–960. doi:10.1007/s11422-011- 9349-z

Carroll, R. (1997). *Sugar in the raw: Voices of young Black girls in America.* New York, NY: Three Rivers Press.

CBS Chicago. (2014, January 1). *Police: Chicago reports 415 murders in 2013, lowest since 1965.* Retrieved from http://chicago.cbslocal.com/2014/01/01/police-chicago-reports-415-murders-in-2013-lowest-since-1965/

Centers for Disease Control and Prevention. (2010). *CDC study finds U.S. herpes rates remain high.* Retrieved from http://www.cdc.gov/nchhstp/Newsroom/hsv2pressrelease.html

Chang, T., & Williams, E. (2011, February 8). Your turn: Give parents more power in schools. *The Root.* Retrieved from http://www.theroot.com/views/your-turn-give-parents-more-power-schools

Chicago Public Schools. (2014a). *Stats and facts.* Retrieved from http://cps.edu/About_CPS/At-a-glance/Pages/Stats_and_facts.aspx

Chicago Public Schools. (2014b). *Chicago public schools fiscal year 2014 budget.* Retrieved from http://cps.edu/finance/FY14budget/pages/revenue.aspx

Cholke, S. (2015a, June 30). Survey ranks CPS teaching at the top, family involvement at the bottom. *DNAinfo.* Retrieved from http://www.dnainfo.com/chicago/20150630/hyde-park/survey-ranks-cps-teaching-at-top-family-involvement-at-bottom

Cholke, S. (2015b, June 30). 'Army of Moms' starts patrolling south side after shooting. *DNAinfo.* Retrieved from http://www.dnainfo.com/chicago/20150630/englewood/army-of-moms-starts-patrolling-englewood-after-shooting

Christian, B. (1985). *Black feminist criticism.* New York, NY: Routledge.

Chua, A. (2011). *Battle Hymn of the tiger mother.* London, England: The Penguin Press HC.

Clandinin, D. J., & Connelly, F. M. (2000). *Narrative inquiry: Experience and story in qualitative research.* San Francisco, CA: Jossey Bass Publishers.

Clark Hine, D., & Thompson, K. (1999). *A shining thread of hope: The history of Black women in America.* New York, NY: Broadway Books.

Cleage, P. (1994). *Deals with the devil: And other reasons to riot.* New York, NY: Ballantine Books.

Clemons, K. M. (2014). I've got to do something for my people: Black women teachers of the 1964 Mississippi freedom schools. *Western Journal of Black Studies, 38*(3), 141–154.

Cliff, M. (1980). *Claiming an identity they taught me to despise.* Cambridge, MA: Persephone Press.

Cliff, M. (1995). If I could write this in fire, I would write this in fire. In A. Biddle (Ed.), *Global voices: Contemporary literature from the non-Western world* (pp. 68–81). Englewood Cliffs, NJ: Prentice Hall. (Original work published in 1985)

Coates, T. (2014). The case for reparations. *The Atlantic.* Retrieved from http://www.theatlantic.com/features/archive/2014/05/the-case-for-reparations/361631

Coates, T. (2015). *Between the world and me.* New York, NY: Spiegle & Grau.

Coffey, A., & Atkinson, P. (1996). *Making sense of qualitative data.* Thousand Oaks, CA: Sage.

Comer, J. P., & Haynes, N. M. (1991). Meeting the needs of Black children in public schools: A school reform challenge. In C. V. Willie, A. Garibaldi, & W. L. Reed (Eds.), *The education of African-Americans* (pp. 67–71). New York, NY: Auburn House.

Common & Bradley, A. (2011). *One day it'll all make sense.* New York, NY: Atria Books.

Connelly, F. M., & Clandinin, D. J. (1990). Stories of experience and narrative inquiry. *Educational Researcher, 19*(5), 2–14.

Cooper, C. W. (2005). School choice and the standpoint of African American mothers: Considering the power of positionality. *The Journal of Negro Education, 2*(74), 174–189.

Cooper, C. W., & McCoy, S. Z. (2009). Poverty and African American mothers: Countering biased ideologies, representations, and the politics of containment. *Journal of the Association for Research on Mothering, 11*(2), 47–57.

Crenshaw, K. (1989). Demarginalizing the intersection of race and sex: A Black feminist critique of antidiscrimination doctrine, feminist theory, and antiracist politics. *University of Chicago Legal Form,* 139–167.

Creswell, J. (2008). *Educational research: Planning, conducting, and evaluating quantitative and qualitative research*. Upper Saddle River, NJ: Pearson.

Crute, S. (2010, April 20). Behind the herpes numbers. *The Root*. Retrieved from http://www.theroot.com/views/behind-herpes-numbers

Curry, C., & Martinez, L. (2014, August 14). Ferguson police's show of force highlights militarization of America's cops. *ABC News*. Retrieved from http://abcnews.go.com/US/ferguson-police-small-army-thousands-police-departments/story?id=24977299

Dates, J., & Barlow, W. (Eds.). (1993). *Split image: African Americans in the mass media* (2nd ed.). Washington, DC: Howard University Press.

Davis, A. Y. (1990). *Women, culture and politics*. New York, NY: Vintage Books. (Original work published in 1989)

Davis, A. Y. (1993). Outcast mothers and surrogates: Racism and reproductive health in the nineties. In L. S. Kauffman (Ed.), American feminist thought at century's end (pp. 1–26). Cambridge, MA: Blackwell.

Davis, K. (Director). (2005). *A girl like me* [Short motion picture]. United States: Reel Works Teen Filmmaking.

Delgado, J. (2013, January 30). Girl who performed at Obama inaugural events slain on South Side. *The Chicago Tribune*. Retrieved from http://articles.chicagotribune.com/2013-01-30/news/chi-2-shot-at-or-near-south-side-high-school-20130129_1_inaugural-events-small-park-students

Delgado, R., & Stefancic, J. (2001). *Critical race theory: An introduction*. New York, NY: New York University Press.

Desilver, D. (2014, July 14). Despite recent shootings, Chicago nowhere near U.S. 'murder capital.' *Pew Research Center*. Retrieved from http://www.pewresearch.org/fact-tank/2014/07/14/ despite-recent-shootings-chicago-nowhere-near-u-s-murder-capital/

Dickson, M. (1988). *Slipping the bond: A narrative inquiry of women elementary educators in leadership roles* (Unpublished manuscript).

Dillard, C. B. (2000). The substance of things hoped for, the evidence of things not seen: Examining and endarkened feminist epistemology in educational research and leadership. *International Journal of Qualitative Studies in Education, 13*(6), 661–681.

Dillard, C. B. (2008). Re-membering culture: Bearing witness to the spirit of identity in research. *Race and Ethnicity in Education, 11*(1), 87–93.

Douglas, S. J., & Michaels, M. W. (2004). *The mommy myth: The idealization of motherhood and how it has undermined all women*. New York, NY: Free Press.

DuBois, W. E. B. (1903). *The souls of Black folk*. New York, NY: Bantam Books.

Duncan, A. (2010, July). *The quiet revolution*. Speech given at the National Press Club, Washington, DC. Retrieved from http://www.ed.gov/news/speeches/quiet-revolution-secretary-arne-duncans-remarks-national-press-club

Elejalde-Ruiz, A. (2015, July 16). Starbucks to open store and training site in Englewood. *Chicago Tribune*. Retrieved from http://www.chicagotribune.com/business/breaking/ct-starbucks-englewood-0716-biz-20150715-story.html

Emdin, C. (2010). Affiliation and alienation: Hip-hop, rap, and urban science education. *Journal of Curriculum Studies, 42*(1), 1–25.

Epstein, J. L. (Ed.). (2009). *School, family, and community partnerships: Your handbook for action* (3rd ed.). Thousand Oaks, CA: Corwin Press.

Erbentraut, J. (2015, July 7). Mothers helped troubled stay shooting-free during violent Chicago weekend. *Huffington Post*. Retrieved from http://www.huffingtonpost.com/2015/07/07/moms-on-patrol-chicago-englewood_n_7746672.html

Evans-Winters, V. (2011). *Teaching Black girls: Resiliency in urban classrooms*. New York, NY: Peter Lang. (Original work published in 2005)

Fields-Smith, C. (2005). African American parents before and after Brown. *Journal of Curriculum and Supervision, 20*, 129–135.

Fields-Smith, C. (2007). Social class and African-American parental involvement In J. Van Galen & G. W. Noblit (Eds.), *Late to class: Social class and schooling in the new economy* (pp. 167–202). New York, NY: State University of New York Press.

Fitzpatrick, L., & Golab, A. (2013, March 7). Black students most likely to have their school on CPS closure list. *Chicago Sun-Times.* Retrieved from http://www.suntimes.com/news/education/18626817-418/black-students-far-more-likely-to-see-their-cps-school-closed-than-others-sun-times-analysis.html#.VI CWx769Txg

Foley, D. E. (1997). Deficit thinking models based on culture: The anthropological protest. In R. Valencia (Ed.), *The evolution of deficit thinking: Educational thought and practice* (pp. 113–131). London, England: Falmer.

Friedan, B. (1963). *The feminine mystique.* New York, NY: W.W. Norton and Company.

Freire, P. (2000). *Pedagogy of the oppressed.* New York, NY: Continuum International Publishing Group. (Original work published in 1970)

Gates, H. L., & McKay, N. Y. (Eds.). (1997). *The Norton anthology of African American literature.* New York, NY: W. W. Norton & Company.

Generett, G. G., & Jeffries, R. B. (Eds.). (2003). *Black women in the field: Experiences understanding ourselves and others through qualitative research.* Cresskill, NJ: Hampton Press.

Giddings, P. (1984). *When and where I enter: The impact of Black women on race and sex in America.* New York, NY: William Murrow.

Gilman, S. (1985). Black bodies, White bodies: Toward an iconography of female sexuality in late nineteenth century art, medicine, and literature. In H. L. Gates (Ed.), *Race, writing, and difference.* Chicago, IL: University of Chicago Press.

Grothman, G., & Wisconsin senator. (2012, March 2). Proposes law that declares single parenthood child abuse. *Huffington Post.* Retrieved from http://www.huffingtonpost.com/2012/03/02/glenn-grothman-wisconsin-law-single-parenthood-child-abuse_n_1316834.html

Glesne, C. (1997). That rare feeling: Re-presenting through poetic transcription. *Qualitative Inquiry, 2,* 202–221.

Glesne, C. (2006). *Becoming qualitative researchers: An introduction* (3rd ed.). Boston, MA: Allyn & Bacon.

Gonzalez, N., Moll, L. C., & Amanti, C. (Eds). (2005). *Funds of knowledge: Theorizing practices in households, communities, and classrooms.* New York, NY: Routledge.

Goodall, H. L. (2000). *Writing the new ethnography.* Oxford, England: AltaMira Press.

Grande, S. (2004). *Red pedagogy: Native American social and political thought.* New York, NY: Rowman & Littlefield Publishers, Inc.

Grant, J. (1998). *Raising baby by the book: The education of American mothers.* New Haven, CT: Yale University Press.

Grant, T. (2010, March 9). Study finds median wealth for single black women at $5. *Pittsburgh Post-Gazette.* Retrieved from http://www.post-gazette.com/pg/10068/1041225-84.stm

Greenlee, S. (1989). *The spook who sat by the door.* Detroit, MI: Wayne State University Press. (Original work published in 1969)

Groves, P. (2003). Insider, outsider, or exotic other? Identity, performance, reflexivity, and postcritical ethnography. In G. G. Generett & R. B. Jeffries (Eds.), *Black women in the field: Experiences understanding ourselves and others through qualitative research* (pp. 103–115). Cresskill, NJ: Hampton Press.

Haile Selassie, I. (n.d.). In *Encyclopædia Britannica online.* Retrieved from http://www.britannica.com/EBchecked/topic/251817/Haile-Selassie-I

Hancock, A. (2004). *The politics of disgust: The public identity of the welfare queen.* New York, NY: New York University Press.

Harris-Perry, M. V. (2011). *Sister citizen: Shame, stereotypes, and Black women in America: For colored girls who've considered politics when being strong isn't enough.* New Haven, NJ: Yale University Press.

Hartsock, N. (1983). The feminist standpoint. In S. Harding & M. B. Hintikka (Eds.), *Discovering reality* (pp. 283–310). Boston, MA: D. Reidel Publishing Company.

Heller, J. (1972, July 26). Syphilis victims in U.S. study went untreated for 40 years. *The New York Times*, pp. 1 column 2, 8 column 1.

Herrnstein, R. J., & Murray, C. A. (1996). *The bell curve: Intelligence and class structure in American life*. New York, NY: Simon & Schuster.

Higginbotham, E. (1985). *Employment for professional black women in the twentieth century*. Memphis, TN: Center for Research on Women.

Hill-Collins, P. (1995). The social construction of black feminist thought. In B. Guy-Sheftall (Ed.), *Words of fire: An anthology of African American feminist thought* (pp. 338–357). New York, NY: The New Press. (Original work published in 1989)

Hill-Collins, P. (2004a). Shifting the center: Race, class, and feminist theorizing about motherhood. In E. N. Glenn, G. Chang, & L. R. Forcey (Eds.), *Mothering: Ideology, experience, and agency* (pp. 45–66). New York, NY: Routledge.

Hill-Collins, P. (2004b). Get your freak on: Sex, babies and images of Black femininity. In P. Hill-Collins (Ed.), *Black sexual politics: African Americans, gender, and the new racism* (pp. 119–148). New York, NY: Routledge.

Hill-Collins, P. (2009). *Black feminist thought: Knowledge, consciousness, and the politics of empowerment*. New York, NY: Routledge. (Original work published 1990)

Holloway, L. (2011, February 24). New York latest target of Black anti-abortion billboards. *The Root*. Retrieved from http://www.theroot.com/views/re-ppnyc-statement-abortion-billboard-targeting-african-americans-nyc

hooks, b. (1981). *Ain't I a woman: Black women and feminism*. Boston, MA: South End.

hooks, b. (2014, November). Keynote address presented at the *National Women's Studies Association Annual Conference*, San Juan, Puerto Rico.

Hull, G. T., Bell-Scott, P., & Smith, B. (1982). *All the women are White, all the Blacks are men, but some of us are brave: Black women's studies*. Old Westbury, NY: Feminist Press.

Hurston, Z. N. (1995). In C. Wall (Ed.), *Zora Neal Hurston: Folklore, memoirs, and other writings: Mules and men, tell my horse, dust tracks on a road, selected articles*. New York, NY: Library of America.

Jacob, I. (Ed.). (2002). *My sisters' voices: Teenage girls of color speak out*. New York, NY: Henry Holt and Company.

Jeffries, R. B. (2003). "I yam what I am": Examining qualitative research through the ethnographic self, the literary "other," and the academy. In G. G. Generett & R. B. Jeffries (Eds.), *Black women in the field: Experiences understanding ourselves and others through qualitative research* (pp. 129–144). Cresskill, NJ: Hampton Press.

Jenkins Schwartz, M. (2010). *Birthing a slave: Motherhood and medicine in the antebellum South*. Cambridge, MA: Harvard University Press.

Jenson, T. (2010, April 13). Black arts movement poet Carolyn M. Rodgers. *The Chicago Tribune*. Retrieved from http://articles.chicagotribune.com/2010-04-13/features/ct-met-0414-rodgers-obit-20100413_1_black-arts-movement-black-women-black-literature

Johnson, K. P. (2013). *No fear for freedom: The story of the friendship 9*. York, SC: Simply Creative Works.

Johnson, M. (2013, September 26). Chicago not actually 'Murder capital' of, well, anything. *CBS Chicago*. Retrieved from http://chicago.cbslocal.com/2013/09/26/chicago-not-actually-murder-capital-of-well-anything/

Jones, J. (2009). *Labor of love, labor of sorrow: Black women, work, and the family from slavery to the present*. New York, NY: Basic Books.

Jones, J. H. (1993). *Bad blood: The Tuskegee syphilis experiment*. New York, NY: The Free Press.

Kasperkevic, J. (2015, February 3). In gentrified cities which came first: Starbucks or higher real estate prices? *The Guardian*. Retrieved from http://www.theguardian.com/money/us-money-blog/2015/feb/03/starbucks-gentrification-real-estate-prices

Kerlin, B. A. (2000). Qualitative research in the United States. *Forum: Qualitative Social Research, 1*(1). Retrieved from http://qualitative-research.net/fqs

Kilgour Dowdy, J., & Wynne, J. T. (Eds.). (2005). *Racism, research, and educational reform: Voices from the city.* New York, NY: Peter Lang.

King, J., & Mitchell, C. A. (1990). *Black mothers to sons: Juxtaposing African American literature with social practice.* New York, NY: Peter Lang.

Klimas, L. (2012, June 25). Makes very little sense: Why are army tanks rolling down residential roads for training in St. Louis? *The Blaze.* Retrieved from http://www.theblaze.com/stories/2012/06/25/makes-very-little-sense-why-are-army-tanks-rolling-down-residential-roads-for-training-in-st-louis/

Kwame Nkrumah. (n.d.). In *Encyclopædia Britannica online.* Retrieved from http://www.britannica.com EBchecked/topic/416674/Kwame-Nkrumah

La Rue, L. (1995). An argument for Black women's liberation as a revolutionary force. In B. Guy-Sheftall (Ed.), *Words of fire: An anthology of African-American feminist thought* (pp. 164–174). New York, NY: The New Press. (Original work published 1970)

Labov, W. (1982). Speech actions and reactions in personal narratives. In D. Tannen (Ed.), *Analyzing discourse: Text and talk* (pp. 219–247). Washington, DC: Georgetown University Press.

Lacks, L., & Lacks, B. (2013). *HeLa family stories: Lawrence and Bobbette.* HeLa Family Enterprise.

Ladd-Taylor, M. (1997). Saving babies and sterilizing mothers: Eugenics and welfare politics in the interwar United States. *Social Politics,* 4(1), 136–153.

Ladner, J. A. (1995). *Tomorrow's tomorrow.* Lincoln, NE: University of Nebraska Press.

Ladson-Billings, G. (1995). Toward a theory of culturally relevant pedagogy. *American Educational Research Journal, 32*(3), 465–491.

Ladson-Billings, G. (2006). From the achievement gap to the education debt: Understanding achievement in U.S. schools. *Educational Researcher, 35*(7), 3–12.

Ladson-Billings, G., & Tate, W. F. (1995). Toward a critical race theory of education. *Teachers College Record, 97*(1), 47–68.

Lareau, A. (2003). *Unequal childhoods: Class, race, and family life.* Berkeley, CA: University of California Press.

Leavy, P. (2009). *Method meets art: Arts-based research practice.* New York, NY: Guilford Press.

Lewis, O. (1959). *Five families: Mexican case studies in the culture of poverty.* New York, NY: Basic Books.

Lorde, A. (2007a). Poetry is not a luxury. In A. Lorde (Ed.), *Sister outsider* (pp. 36–39). Berkeley, CA: Crossing Press. (Original work published 1977)

Lorde, A. (2007b). The master's tools will never dismantle the house. In A. Lorde (Ed.), *Sister outsider* (pp. 110–114). Berkeley, CA: Crossing Press. (Original work published 1979)

Lorde, A. (2007c). The transformation of silence into language and action. In A. Lorde (Ed.), *Sister outsider* (pp. 40–44). Berkeley, CA: Crossing Press. (Original work published 1977)

Love, B. (2012). *Hip hop's li'l sistas speak: Negotiating hip hop identities and politics in the new South.* New York, NY: Peter Lang.

Love, B. (2015, January). *All that hip hop touches, it changes.* Lecture conducted at the Emergent Speakers Series, DePaul University, Chicago, IL.

Lynn, M., & Dixson, A. D. (Eds.). (2013). *Handbook of critical race theory in education.* New York, NY: Routledge.

MacIntyre, A. (1984). *After virtue: A study in moral theory* (2nd ed.). Notre Dame, IN: University of Notre Dame Press.

Madison, D. S. (2011, February). *Critical ethnography.* Lecture conducted from The University of North Carolina, Chapel Hill, NC.

Madison, D. S. (2005). *Critical ethnography: Method, ethics, and performance.* Thousand Oaks, CA: Sage.

Magubane, Z. (2001). Which bodies matter? Feminism, poststructuralism, race, and the curious theoretical Odyssey of the "Hottentot Venus." *Gender and Society, 6*(15), 816–834.

Malinowski, B. (1926). *Crime and custom in savage society.* Lanham, MD: Rowman & Littlefield.

Malinowski, B. (1927). *Sex and repression in savage society.* London, England: Routledge.

Marcus, S. S. (n.d.). The whole world is watching. *Encyclopedia of Chicago*. Retrieved from http://www.encyclopedia.chicagohistory.org/pages/410158.html

Martinez, E. (2009a, September 29). Derrion Albert video shows teens beating Christian Fenger high school student to death. *CBS News*. Retrieved from http://www.cbsnews.com/8301-504083_162-5348755-504083.html

Martinez, E. (2009b, October 9). Derrion Albert beating death: A wake-up call for America. *CBS News*. Retrieved from http://www.cbsnews.com/8301-504083_162-5370998-504083.html

Mather, M. (2010, May). *U.S. children in single-mother families*. Retrieved from http://www.prb.org/pdf10/single-motherfamilies.pdf

McGrath, D. J., & Kuriloff, P. J. (1999). They're going to tear the doors off this place: Upper-middle-class parent school involvement and the educational opportunity of other people's children. *Educational Policy, 13*, 603–629.

McNeil, S., Harris-McKoy, D., Brantley, C., Fincham, F., & Beach, S. R. H. (2014). Middle class African American mothers' depressive symptoms mediate perceived discrimination and reported child externalizing behaviors. *Journal of Child and Family Studies, 23*, 381–388.

Mental Health America. (n.d.). *African American communities and mental health*. Alexandria, VA. Retrieved from http://www.mentalhealthamerica.net/african-american-mental-health

Merriam, S. (1991). How research produces knowledge. In J. M. Peters & P. Jarvis (Eds.), *Adult education: Evolution and achievements in a developing field of study* (pp. 42–65). San Francisco, CA: Jossey-Bass.

Moore, K. T. J. (2005). *Glimpse of our journey: Black women's political activisms in Chicago's tenement housing projects* (Unpublished master's thesis). Pullman, WA: Washington State University.

Moore, K. T. J. (2009). *She who learns teachers: Black women teachers of the 1963 Mississippi freedom schools* (Doctoral dissertation). Retrieved from the UNC-Chapel Hill Libraries online database website: http://dc.lib.unc.edu/u?/etd,2264

Morgan, J. (1999). *When chickenheads come home to root: A hip-hop feminist breaks it down*. New York, NY: Simon & Schuster.

Morrison, T. (2008). In C. C. Denard (Ed.), *What moves at the margin: Selected nonfiction*. Jackson, MS: University Press of Mississippi.

Murray, C. A. (1984). *Losing ground: American social policy, 1950–1980*. New York, NY: Basic Books.

Myerson, H. (2012, September 14). Chicago chooses sides. *The American Prospect*. Retrieved from http://prospect.org/article/chicago-chooses-sides

Noblit, G. W. (1999). *Particularities: Collected essays on ethnography and education*. New York, NY: Peter Lang.

Omolade, B. (1994). *The rising song of African American women*. New York, NY: Routledge.

Patton, M. Q. (2001). *Qualitative research and evaluation methods* (3rd ed.). Thousand Oaks, CA: Sage Publications.

Payne, R. (1995). *A Framework: Understanding and working with students and adults from poverty*. Highlands, TX: Aha Process, Inc.

Perry, T., Steele, C., & Hilliard III, A. (2004). *Young, gifted, and Black: Promoting high achievement among African-American students*. Boston, MA: Beacon Press.

Peter, L. J. (1981). *Peter's people and their marvelous ideas*. Tower & Leisure Sales Company.

Rascoff, S. (2015, March 5). The starbucks effect: How lattes perk up home prices. *LinkedIn*. Retrieved from https://www.linkedin.com/pulse/starbucks-effect-how-lattes-perk-up-home-prices-spencer-rascoff

Reinharz, S. (1992). *Feminist methods in social research*. London, England: Oxford University Press.

Roberts, D. (1997). *Killing the Black body: Race, reproduction, and the meaning of liberty*. New York, NY: Vintage Books.

Robertson, C. (2014). South Carolina judge vacates conviction of George Stinney in 1944 execution. *The New York Times*. Retrieved from http://www.nytimes.com/2014/12/18/us/judge-vacates-conviction-in-1944-execution.html?_r=0

Robnett, B. (2000). *How long? How long? African-American women in the struggle for civil rights*. New York, NY: Oxford University Press.

Rock, R., & Graham, V. (2009). *Mama Rock's rules: Ten lessons for raising a household of successful children*. New York, NY: Harper Paperbacks.

Rossi, R. (2012, February 22). Board of education OKs shake-ups for 17 schools. *Chicago Sun-Times*. Retrieved from http://www.suntimes.com/news/politics/10815524-418/board-of-ed-oks-shake-ups-for-17-schools.html

Sankofa Waters, B. (2015). Oh, you'll be back: Bridging identities of race, gender, poet and community allegiance in academic research. In V. Evans-Winters & B. Love (Eds.), *Endarkened feminist knowledge: Black women speak back, up, & out* (pp. 173–182). New York, NY: Peter Lang.

Schulte, S. (2015, July 7). What worked in Englewood? No shootings over July 4. *ABC 7 Chicago*. Retrieved from http://abc7chicago.com/news/what-worked-in-englewood/833983/

Senate Bill 507. (2012). Wisconsin.

Shakur, A. (1987). *Assata: An autobiography*. Chicago, IL: Lawrence Hill Books.

Skloot, R. (2011). *The immortal life of Henrietta Lacks*. New York, NY: Broadway books.

Smith, B. (Ed.). (2000). *Home girls: A Black feminist anthology*. New Brunswick, NJ: Rutgers University Press. (Original work published 1983)

Staples, R. (1981). The myth of the Black matriarchy. *Black Scholar, 12*(6), 26–34. (Original work published 1970)

Stanfield, J. H. (1985). The ethnocentric basis of social science knowledge production. *Review of Research in Education, 12*(1), 387–415.

Story, K. A. (2014). *Patricia Hill Collins: Reconceiving motherhood*. Bradford, ON: Demeter Press.

Syler, R. (2008). *Good enough mother: The perfectly imperfect book of parenting*. New York, NY: Gallery Books.

Taylor, E., Gillborn, D., & Ladson-Billings, G. (Eds.). (2009). *Foundations of critical race theory in education*. New York, NY: Routledge.

The Gambia. (n.d.). In *Encyclopædia Britannica online*. Retrieved from http://www.britannica.com/EBchecked/topic/224771/The-Gambia#toc54951

The Law and Policy Group, Incorporated. (2008). *Report on the status of Black women and girls*. New York, NY: Gloria J. Browne-Marshall.

The White House, Office of the Press Secretary. (2013). *Press briefing by press secretary Jay Carney, 1/30/13* [Press release]. Retrieved from http://www.whitehouse.gov/the-press-office/2013/01/30/press-briefing-press-secretary-jay-carney-13013

University of Chicago Consortium on School Research. (2014). *5 Essentials school reports*. Chicago, IL. Retrieved from https://cps.5-essentials.org/2014/

U.S. Census Bureau. (2010). *American factfinder fact sheet*. Chicago, IL. Retrieved from http://factfinder2.census.gov/faces/nav/jsf/pages/index.xhtml

U.S. Department of Education. (2006). *The adult lives of at-risk students: The roles of attainment and engagement in high school (NCES 2006-328)*. Washington, DC: J. D. Finn.

U.S. Department of Health and Human Services. (1979). *The Belmont report (Human subjects research 45 CFR 46)*. Retrieved from http://www.hhs.gov/ohrp/humansubjects/guidance/belmont.html

U.S. Department of Labor. (1965). *The Negro family: A case for national action*. Washington, DC: D. P. Moynihan.

Villenas, S. (1996). The colonizer/colonized Chicana ethnographer: Identity, marginalization, and co-optation in the field. *Harvard Educational Research, 66*(4), 711–4731.

Walker, A. (1983). *In search of our mothers' gardens: Womanist prose*. San Diego, CA: Harcourt Brace & Company.

Walker, V. S. (1996). *Their highest potential: An African American school community in the segregated South*. Chapel Hill, NC: University of North Carolina Press.

Walker, V. S. (2000). Valued segregated schools for African American children in the South, 1935–1969: A review of common themes and characteristics. *Review of Educational Research, 70*, 253–286.

Walton, Q. L., & Shepard Payne, J. (2015). *Missing the mark: Cultural expressions of depressive symptoms among African American women and men* (Unpublished manuscript).

West, C. (2003). A genealogy of modern racism. In L. Cahoone (Ed.), *From modernism to postmodernism* (pp. 298–309). Malden, MA: Blackwell Publishing. (Original work published 1982)

Whitehead, J. W. (2013, November 18). Drones, tanks, and grenade launchers: Coming soon to a police department near you. *Huffington post*. Retrieved from http://www.huffingtonpost.com/ john-w-whitehead/police-military-equipment_b_4296948.html

Whitehead, K. (2015). *Letters to my Black sons: Raising boys in a post-racial America*. Baltimore, MD: Apprentice House.

Williams, H. (2007). *Self-taught: African American education in slavery and freedom*. Chapel Hill, NC: University of North Carolina Press.

Wing, A. (Ed.). (2003). *Critical race feminism: A reader*. New York, NY: New York University Press. (Original work published 1997)

Yosso, T. J. (2005). Whose culture has capital? A critical race theory discussion of community cultural wealth. *Race Ethnicity and Education, 8*(1), 69–91.

Zavadski, K. (2014, December 4). 25 activities Black people should avoid around cops. *New York Magazine*. Retrieved from http://nymag.com/daily/intelligencer/2014/12/25-things-black-people-shouldnt-do-around-cops.html

ABOUT THE AUTHOR

Chicago native **Billye Sankofa Waters**, Ph.D., is an interdisciplinary scholar trained in Writing, Black World Studies, Education, and Women's Studies. In addition to *We Can Speak for Ourselves,* she is the author of *Penetrated Soul* (2002). She is an Assistant Teaching Professor in the Graduate School of Education at Northeastern University. She serves as the Founding Director of Sunflower Seeds Studio and is a member of Delta Sigma Theta Sorority, Inc., as well as several other academic and professional organizations. For life balance, she enjoys blogging, photography, and curating art/memorabilia for the Sankofa Waters' Studio. For more information, visit: www.drsankofawaters.com.

NAME INDEX

SUBJECT INDEX

21st Century, 9, 83, 94

A

Abortion, 54

administrator/administration, 5, 6, 8, 15n14, 22, 26, 39, 42, 53, 60–62, 64, 66, 70, 72, 73, 84–86, 88

African Diaspora, 15n1, 15n17

arts, 6, 11, 38, 55, 62, 80, 109, 122

at-risk, 30, 111, 112

B

beauty, xiv, 1, 10, 18

becoming mother, 47–49, 54, 55, 73, 74

behavior, 6, 10, 30, 35, 63, 73, 79, 83–87, 103, 106, 107

   appropriate, 23

   correct behavior, 68, 69

being vocal, 37, 66, 67

Belmont Report, The, 35

Black feminism, xiii, xiv, 10, 12, 19, 110

Black on Black crime, 15n3, 101

Black on Black Love, 2, 15n3

blended family, 71, 74, 75, 77

blog/social media, xvi, 14, 39, 40, 100, 103, 104, 109, 111

   Facebook, 76, 104

   For Harriet, 104

   Twitter, 104

   YouTube, 5

Brown V. Board, 20, 90n1

C

care, xi, xvi, 3, 6, 11, 13, 14, 15n6, 26, 31, 39, 46, 50–53, 58, 60, 62–64, 68, 70, 79–81, 85, 95, 98n3, 99, 103, 106, 119

Catholic (religion), 3, 30, 46, 68, 79, 115

cheer, 45–47

Chicago neighborhoods, 102

   Englewood, 101, 102

   Jeffery Manor, xiv

Chiraq, 101

choice, xiii, 6, 21, 26, 27, 32, 45, 51, 54, 58, 60–62, 64, 68, 71, 74, 77, 79, 83, 88, 89, 117

Civil Rights, 13, 15n5, 30, 32, 69, 99, 100

Clair Huxtable, 106, 107

coding, 36, 37

cognitive dissonance, 108

communication, xix, 7, 8, 14, 21, 22, 26, 39, 58, 60, 61, 75, 84–88, 95, 99, 104, 109

community/communities, xi, xx, 1–5, 7, 9, 10, 12, 14, 15n3, 16n15, 19, 20, 22, 24–27, 29, 31, 33, 35, 36, 40–42, 45, 46, 57–60, 71, 73–75, 77n1, 79–82, 85, 90, 91n1, 95, 96, 101–104, 106, 108, 110, 112, 113, 117–119

concerted cultivation, 72, 81, 86

controlling images, xi, xv, 1, 10, 19, 24, 25, 109, 110

   baby mama, 94, 99

   Bad Black Mother (BBM), 12, 86

   bitch, 11, 56, 60, 86–88, 99

   Buck, 109

   crackwhore, 94

   Jezebel, 10–12, 94

   Magical Negro, 43n2

   Mammy, 10, 11, 31, 94, 99, 109

   Sapphire, 10, 11, 88, 94, 107

   Welfare Queen, 8, 11, 16n20, 30, 94